MY LIFE LESSONS

MY LIFE LESSONS

An Intellectual Journey

LEE-JAY CHO

HAWAI'I ASIA-PACIFIC INSTITUTE
Honolulu

Printed in the United States of America

First printing, 2026

Library of Congress Cataloging-in-Publication Data

Names: Cho, Lee-Jay author
Title: My life lessons : an intellectual journey / Lee-Jay Cho.
Other titles: Intellectual journey
Description: Honolulu : Hawaiʻi Asia-Pacific Institute, 2026.
Identifiers: LCCN 2025008589 | ISBN 9781952460081 cloth
Subjects: LCSH: Cho, Lee-Jay | East Asia specialists—Biography | International relations specialists—Biography | LCGFT: Autobiographies
Classification: LCC DS32.7.C46 A3 2025 | DDC 327.1092 [B]—dcundefined
LC record available at https://lccn.loc.gov/2025008589

Hawaiʻi Asia-Pacific Institute books are printed on acid-free paper and meet the guidelines for permanence and durability of the Council on Library Resources.

Distributed by University of Hawaiʻi Press
2840 Kolowalu Street
Honolulu, HI 96822–1888

To tomorrow's Young Leaders

Contents

Foreword

I am deeply honored and humbled to write this foreword for the memoir of a great man, Dr. Lee-Jay Cho. He was a man of many dimensions. Some will remember him as a scholar—one of the pioneers in the field of demography and population studies. Others will recall him as an educator with a vast network of students across Asia and America. Many remember his profound imprint as Vice President and Acting President of the East-West Center (EWC) during a pivotal era when the world sought to understand the "East Asian Miracle," and later, to navigate the aftermath of Japan's economic bubble. He established and directed the Population Institute, attracting renowned scholars who advanced innovative population accounting and modeling methods to support policy and planning. Generations of Northeast Asia Economic Forum (NEAEF) "Young Leaders" will remember him as a nurturing father figure who spoke many languages and brought peers together across the region to collaborate on matters of global consequence. Senior NEAEF leaders—including governors, ministers, ambassadors, academics, and executives—will remember substantive conferences in rare locations that fostered meaningful collaborations and enduring peace. Through all of this, Dr. Cho remained a devoted Christian, husband, father, and grandfather—deeply committed to family and faith.

I was profoundly blessed to witness many of these dimensions and to become his dear friend. It was in 1993 that I first came to Honolulu as a young assistant professor at the University of Hawai'i at Mānoa (UH Mānoa). Early on, upon the invitation of another great mentor, Dr. Seiji Naya, I held a visiting position at the neighboring EWC within the International Economics and Politics Division. As EWC Vice President, Dr. Cho was a dynamic and, at times, intimidating force. The EWC faced defining choices then: would it pull toward the U.S. Department of State as an American think tank, or stand among Asia's leading scholarly institutes as a network of international collaboration? Drs. Naya and Cho both believed that any funding from Washington, D.C., should be matched—or exceeded—by contributions from Asia and the Pacific. They saw in the East Asian Miracle lessons for development that could extend to Africa, Latin America, and beyond.

In 1991, Dr. Cho established his own nonprofit enterprise, the Hawai'i Asia-Pacific Institute (HAPI), with a mission to promote international exchange and understanding in population and economic development. In 2013, he formally registered the tradename Northeast Asia Economic Forum (NEAEF), with HAPI serving as its secretariat. As the EWC grew increasingly oriented toward Washington, Dr. Cho channeled his passion and energy into HAPI and NEAEF—institutions that reflected his lifelong belief in the power of dialogue and cooperation.

My own life followed a parallel path. Academically, I rose through the ranks to become a full professor of economics. My expertise in international trade led me to consulting roles with the World Bank and governments across the Middle East and North Africa. Later, I was called into executive leadership at UH Mānoa—as department chair, associate vice chancellor, chancellor, and eventually, dean of the College of Social Sciences. It was during my administrative years that I became closest to Dr. Cho. We partnered on many initiatives, co-sponsored countless activities, and developed a deep friendship grounded in shared convictions about globalization, economics, and peace.

Dr. Cho was only slightly younger than my father, Roy Eby, and I often reflected on the parallels between their lives. Dr. Cho's youth, as this memoir recounts, was shaped by war. He was forced to navigate among peoples in conflict, witnessing firsthand the injustices and brutality of division. Yet he discovered, through faith and perseverance, that mutual respect and understanding were possible. Though he rose from poverty to achieve an elite American education, his heart remained with the Korean people and with all those in the region. He believed that love among peoples could transcend hostility—and that peace could emerge through practical cooperation. For Dr. Cho, economics was not merely theory, but a pathway to reconciliation.

My father held a similar worldview. As a Mennonite farmer in Lancaster County, Pennsylvania, Roy Eby was raised in the pacifist tradition. The Great Depression brought hardship to my father's family, but his intellect carried him to college and graduate studies in mathematics at the University of Chicago—the same institution where Dr. Cho earned his PhD in sociology. When drafted, my father declared as a conscientious objector and served in Vietnam and Taiwan in alternative service. There, he, too, witnessed the devastations of war, deepening his devotion to peace, nonviolence, and international understanding. His life, like Dr. Cho's, was rooted in faith and a profound respect for humanity, regardless of nationality, ethnicity, or station in life.

As a trade economist and a Mennonite farmer's daughter, I resonated deeply with Dr. Cho's vision. Through HAPI and NEAEF, I contributed my own networks and commitments, engaging UH Mānoa students in his programs. Some of my most gifted students worked as interns, volunteers, and participants in the NEAEF Young Leaders Program (YLP).

What makes NEAEF remarkable is its courage. The region it encompasses—Japan, China, Korea, Mongolia, and Russia—has long been marked by war, competition, and deep-seated tensions. Dr. Cho was putting into action his vision for a peaceful region that could be achieved as friends and colleagues work together across national borders and with common purpose. Dr. Cho personally experienced the bitterness and mistrust that persist today, yet he never lost faith in the possibility of peace. It is no small act of bravery to establish and sustain an organization devoted to economic cooperation, mutual understanding, and regional peace across these nations. Under his leadership, NEAEF has produced genuine collaborations, enduring friendships, and tangible progress toward harmony.

My father passed away in October 2020, and Dr. Cho soon thereafter. Their near-simultaneous departures were deeply personal losses. At Dr. Cho's service, I shared these spontaneous words:

"It's hard to find the words. I'll be laying my own father to rest tomorrow, so this is an especially precious moment for me. I want to say how wonderful it was to work with Dr. Lee-Jay Cho—how inspiring he was, and how he truly brought out the best in us. I want his family to know that he worked well past the age when most would retire. He had a mission and a vision. His youth was spent in conflict—in Japan and Korea—where he saw much hardship and cruelty. Yet from that, he shaped a vision that I embraced wholeheartedly: that through economic relations, people who might otherwise be divided could find common purpose, and that cooperation could become a path to peace. He believed it was essential to help the next generation understand this. Even amid the pandemic, he continued leading the NEAEF Young

Leaders Program because he believed that when people from different backgrounds and beliefs come together—to work, share meals, and learn from one another—peace can grow from fellowship. In this time of division, his vision remains brilliant and vital. His legacy endures in all of us who had the privilege to work with him. He was a man of wisdom, compassion, and faith who turned adversity into joy. That joy will carry his legacy far into the future. My deepest condolences to his beloved family, whom I appreciate very much."

Dr. Cho valued his friends and family deeply. He sought out those willing to dedicate themselves to his mission and nurtured those relationships with warmth and loyalty. Anyone fortunate enough to be part of his circle felt an enduring bond with him—and with one another. I continue to be moved by how powerfully his expectations still inspire action. Long after his passing, his vision and legacy continue to guide me, and I am joined in this by many colleagues and leaders across the Pacific. It has been a true honor to step into the role of President of the Hawai'i Asia-Pacific Institute and the Northeast Asia Economic Forum, and I am grateful that Dr. Cho's legacy continues to guide our efforts to this day.

Denise Eby Konan
President, Hawai'i Asia-Pacific Institute
and the Northeast Asia Economic Forum
Honolulu, Hawai'i

INTRODUCTION

Nuy Cho

I want to relay my lifelong curiosity to find out about the inner "Dr. Lee-Jay Cho" and how it relates to the shaping and understanding of this memoir. My father was a bit of a mystery with his history. I did not know many details about my father's early life and how it shaped who he would become. None of us in his immediate family did.

He protected what he held inside like a vault. At a young age, circumstances forced him to sacrifice his youth and spend his life from age twelve and onward supporting his father, mother, and six siblings, and later, to a large degree, his extended family. A house fire destroyed Dad's childhood photos and keepsakes. We don't have evidence of what he looked like as a baby, or of his immediate family, and have had to rely on family and peers to piece together memories.

When I moved back to Honolulu in 2016, I lived near my father until 2020 when he passed away. In March 2020, at the start of the COVID-19 pandemic, my father asked me to help him construct his memoir. The time we spent together on this memoir would end up being the longest period I spent with my father in my adult life. Our relationship prior to this had gone through ebbs and flows of various strains, but with a meaty writing project in front of us and maturity at my side, we were both at our best.

We worked at both my house and at my father's (my old childhood home). Dad would take old newspaper stories written in Korean that he liked and have my mother translate them into English first, before she'd pass them on to me for a more nuanced English version.

We'd talk in English, and Dad would then add anecdotes and reminisce about the past. He would then interject memories and other academic or philosophical notions into them. These sessions would sometimes involve dinners, pleasant interruptions from grandchildren, and teas and desserts served in between.

Throughout the day, my father would call me multiple times to check on my progress with a primary Google Document he was constantly adding pages to. Sometimes he would have an organizational moment and decide to lay a chapter out and then reset the pages. And then we would reconvene, talk again, re-edit, and "so forth" (one of his favorite phrases). We'd meet on the phone or on my lanai—he called it the "COVID Lounge." Sometimes he would show up unexpectedly to tell me something seemingly insignificant about the manuscript, only to get giant hugs from his grandkids.

The way he worked was entirely organic. Some days he would wax poetic about a particular former president he had a relationship with and talk on and on about that person. I would have to sidebar with my mother, Eun-Ja Cho,[1] who is the most knowledgeable about my father's academic or personal affairs, to fact-check.

Then, he would tangentially move on to another story about what happened at a university he may have done a stint or research project at, before starting back on

1. Eun-Ja Cho passed away in early 2025.

about the historical relevance of a statistical theory. This is how my father spoke. I did my best to keep up with him. His purpose with the memoir, he told me, was to educate future generations and young leaders. This is a personal memoir, but one to be shared academically. He was very clear about that.

When my father fell sick in October 2020, he was very close to being finished with this project. He had told me it was nearly complete, and he felt good about where it was at. There were only a few minor chapters to finish that involved a few things he had outlined, and he reported he felt it was in a good place to show my brothers. We talked about a cover photo, and one day I got the one and only photo message I would ever receive from him.

It was a picture of him in black and white, and he looked about 15 years old. No text, just a photo. I wrote back to him asking if he meant to send it to me. I had had no idea he knew how to send a photo text. He barely knew how to use a cell phone. He didn't respond. I phoned him.

I asked, "Dad, did you mean to send me this boyish image of yourself to me?"

He replied, "Yes! That's me!"

I said, "Wow, you are so young!" He chuckled. "I didn't know you knew how to do that, Dad!" He chuckled again.

The pandemic had been hard for him. One of his greatest passions was sharing his knowledge in-person with others. With his annual Young Leaders Program on hold and the Northeast Asia Economic Forum being conducted virtually because of the pandemic in 2020, it was incredibly trying for my dad to not be able to interact with great minds in real life. Being stuck at home for the greater part of the year had been depressing and trying for the avid world traveler.

What he truly loved was being with people and teaching what he knew. Even in the hospital, in his last weeks, we could hear him chomping at the bit, teaching the nursing staff, the aides, anyone around him. He just couldn't help himself. He possessed an incredible desire to show those around him what they could learn.

This memoir is, I hope, a little visit, perhaps, into what it was like to sit down and talk with Dr. Lee-Jay Cho.

Part I

1

MY CHILDHOOD MEMORIES OF THE ASIA PACIFIC WAR

Northeast Asia has experienced both good and troublesome histories. The last two centuries have been afflicted by conflicts, tensions, and wars—in the twentieth century: the Russo-Japanese War, World War II, the Korean War, the Vietnam War, and numerous other conflicts.

I was born in 1936 and lived until nine years of age in Terada in the vicinity of Okubo military airport of Kuse-gun, Kyoto-fu, Japan, geographically located between the cities of Kyoto, Nara, and Osaka. There is a river called Kizugawa that flows south from Nara Prefecture passing through Tanabe on the Osaka-fu side and Terada, on the Kyoto side, toward Osaka, merging into the Yodo River and running through Osaka city to the Pacific Ocean.

Terada was the site of many battles fought during the warring period some five hundred years ago. According to local historical records, Terada castle, in addition to a Ninja community (*of Igashu*), became known as Terada Mura (village), and then Joyo-shi (town).

As a toddler, I suffered from chronic pneumonia and I remember my father taking me on his bicycle to Tanabe across the river to see Dr. Imamura for treatment. With no antibiotics then available, whenever I was deteriorating, I was given transfusions of my mother's blood to resuscitate me, and I was the only one in the family provided with precious cow's milk that was delivered daily.

The year of 1936, my birth year, was marked by the historic 2-2-6 Incident (Niniroku Jiken), an uprising of young imperial Army officers aimed at social justice, intended to cleanse corruption in the government and the military. This mutiny, which had wide support within the military as well as from the public, was quelled by a reluctant Imperial decree. Some one hundred seventy top elite officers with an absolute loyalty to the Emperor were court-martialed and executed. The executions shook the country politically, socially, and morally. Years later, in 1961, General Park Chung Hee, strongly influenced in his Japanese military cadet days by the 2-2-6 Mutiny leaders for social justice, took their spirit and courage to heart and manifested his leadership in the May 16 coup d'état. This was followed by the remarkable economic development symbolized as the "the Miracle on the Han River" during his Presidency.

A few years earlier, in 1931, when Zhang Zolin, China's Warlord in the Northeast region, was assassinated by Japan's Gwandong Army, Japan's incursion into China expanded and its subsequent invasions in Southeast Asia followed. This was known as the Manchurian Incident.

On December 8, 1945, the Japanese Army, led by General Yamashita Tomoyuki, made a surprise attack (synchronized with the Pearl Harbor attack) at Kota Bharu on the east coast of Malaya, invading the Malayan Peninsula in a pretense of liberating it from oppressive British colonial rule.[1]

As a child I saw a propaganda war film entitled *Malay's Harimao* at a movie theater at Momoyama city (where Emperor Meiji's tomb is located), and I was impressed enough to remember the name and the song, originally taken from a

---

1. The attack on Pearl Harbor occurred on December 8, 1941, from the perspective of someone living in Japan.

Malayan tune, adapted for the movie and later rearranged as the Malaysian national anthem *Negaraku.* In the song, a brave young Malay man named Harimao (Tiger) helped the Japanese forces in their cause by his heroic actions. Years later, in Hawai'i, when my family was given a beautiful Shetland Sheepdog puppy, our neighbor's son called out to the dog with the words "Hey tiger," so I gave the dog the name *Hari* (mao) for short, instead of "Tiger."[2]

General Yamashita's army advanced victoriously over the numerically superior British forces to attack Singapore. I was told in my childhood in Japan that in a face-to-face meeting with General Arthur Percival, Commander of the British Forces, on the terms of a truce, Yamashita confronted the British General. Facing the prospect of prolonged arduous street battles, he issued an ultimatum: "Yes-*ka,* No-*ka?*" The bluff worked and Percival surrendered.

Yamashita was highly respected in Japan as a brilliant and courageous general, unlike Tojo Hideki, the Prime Minister, who was General Minister of War at the time. Hideki demoted Yamashita after his Malayan victory and assigned him to a training post in Manchuria. On the Philippine front in 1945, when his close subordinates returned to Japan, Yamashita insisted on remaining to fight beyond the August 15 Japanese surrender in the jungle to face death by hanging, a sentence issued by the War Tribunal in the Philippines. General Percival, having served as a prisoner of war in Manchuria, was invited to observe the sentencing.

On December 8, 1941, Japan made the surprise attack on Pearl Harbor that would culminate in the Pacific War. A couple of years later, as a young school boy, I remember the day when Japan lost Saipan. We were assembled on the school

---

2. Of Japanese descent, Harimao was the son of a barber residing and operating in Malaya then, for the Japanese military. I heard this story when I was in Malaysia (a Post–WWII independent nation, including Singapore, which subsequently seceded, becoming independent, as an advisor in the office of Prime Minister in 1967).

grounds and our principal made a forceful speech stating that the Japanese Forces making a tactical retreat was akin to bending a thin bamboo strip for greater elastic force to hit back at the American enemy. I was in the third grade and the school, by reducing class hours, required its students to collect tea seeds. Each of us was given an individual quota to fill as part of a national mobilization by the defense industry to extract oil, since we were residing in the tea growing region of Uji of Kyoto-fu.

During the Pacific War years, the population in Japan was highly regimented and households had to be strictly accountable. In the entrance of each house, a nameplate had to account for each family member, stating their full name, birth date, and relationship to the head of the household. As an elementary school kid, I used to have this information sewn onto the upper chest of my jacket. This practice was based on a long history of mobilization in countries of the Chinese cultural sphere, including Japan and Korea.

The place where I was born (circa 1980)

Beginning in late 1944, all of us in my neighborhood went through preparation and training in anticipation of American air attacks and eventual invasion. For example, after the warning sirens, we had to stay under a roof, and after the "enemy attack siren," all of us, in protective head covers, were to enter protective dug-in-holes. (It is interesting to reflect that in a pandemic all stay home and in the bombing situation during the war, all stay under the roof or in protective holes.)[3]

As a young boy, I had some frightening experiences watching the War in the air as well as on the ground. Starting in the spring of 1945, "enemy" (American) airplanes were flying over our area and as we approached the summer, with increasing frequency, I could see the American B-29s (built by Boeing) bombing Osaka. Smoke hung over the city like a cloud in the distance. As the days passed, the attacks intensified into saturation bombings in major Japanese cities, starting with Tokyo, Osaka, and Nagoya.

Sometime in July at the Kizu River beach, my friend and I barely avoided being shot by an American P-51 fighter, staying under the surface of the water while the pilot shot the clothes we left on the sand by mistake, taking them for human beings.

Years later in 1959, I was taking evening classes in public administration at George Washington University and I attended a class on public policy taught by Professor E. Brown, Dean of the Graduate School at the time. Brown was elaborating on the term "policy," using his experience as a Navy pilot of an aircraft carrier during WWII in Japan in the summer of 1945, a little before the end of the War. He defined the term "policy" as "what one is allowed to do within its framework," suggesting it was the policy of the

3. This was written during the height of the COVID-19 pandemic, during early to mid-2020.

American Forces to shoot any moving object on the ground in Japan. He explained that he "had never before enjoyed such an exhilarating experience as flying his fighter plane without any restrictions and obstacles, just like driving a truck without any traffic regulation." After his lecture, I told him that fortunately an American fighter pilot had missed me and shot my clothes at Kizu River, and I saw his face freeze with reckoning.

One day in late July 1945, numerous anti-aircraft artillery shells were fired like fireworks at rows of flying B-29 bombers in the sky from Okubo military airport (not too far away, with most of them missing the targets). I watched with fresh eyes as one bomber was hit in the right wing. His plane instantly split and exploded in a burning fire high in the middle of the blue sky, tragically falling into pieces to the ground.

A few days later, in the sky right above my head, I witnessed a crippled American B-29 bomber engage in a dog fight with a Japanese Zero fighter (built by Suzuki, automakers of today). After making one and half vertical cycles, the American pilot ditched into the sandy fields by the Kizu river. There was a sense of "Bravo" for this Zero fighter who appeared from out of nowhere in the midst of absolute American air supremacy at the time.

I got on my bicycle and rode over to the sandy area where the B-29 had crashed. The plane was totally destroyed and shattered asunder. I saw the Japanese Military Police put an American, maybe the pilot, blindfolded with a white cloth, into their vehicle and drive away. At the same time, I watched several Japanese farmers beating the dead bodies of the B-29 crew with their hoes, in flaring vengeance for all the suffering the Americans caused in the war. As a boy, this sight was truly shocking.

As time elapsed day by day, we were harassed by, and suffered from, the long drawn-out rumbling baritone of flying B-29s in group formation and the irritating noise of *Kansaiki,* American fighter planes, strafing over our roofs.

In early August we heard the news that the city of Hiroshima had been hit by a mysteriously vicious bomb, killing a large resident population. This was later confirmed as the first atomic bomb, dropped by a B-29 on August 6, 1945. About a week later, on August 15, I listened together with my family on a static-filled radio, to the voice of the Emperor Showa declaring the unconditional surrender of Japan.

All of us shared trepidation about what would happen to us in our neighborhoods, our towns, and the country after Japan's surrender. Some days later, I happened to take a walk toward a bamboo forest where a space had been created to hide a Japanese training plane. For the first time in my life, I saw a white American in a dark green fatigue outfit who looked serious with a pistol in his hand. I was frightened and walked away from the scene quietly and as fast as I could, imagining a "hairy barbarian" (as propaganda put it) who might harm me.

Weeks passed and a few of us were on the local train (Naraden) to Kyoto. At Momoyama station we saw a bunch of American soldiers in more relaxed outfits. Some took off their shirts in the heat of the summer and they seemed to be constantly eating something in their mouths. We later found they were chewing gum, which we had never seen in Japan.

After the War, Koreans were in a precarious situation. While we were considered Japanese subjects under colonial rule, Koreans had established an out of country provisional government in 1919, first in Shanghai (and later in Chungking), when the Kingdom of Joseon lost its sovereignty in 1910. The Supreme Allied Command (SAC) led by General Douglas MacArthur treated Korea as an ally. Some Koreans in Japan abused their Allied status and perpetrated undesirable and shameful acts that painted lasting images. I remember for about a month after the War, our diet included beef like bulkogi, apparently from Japanese cattle obtained through the Korean connection.

One of the consequences of this situation is the fascinating story of the Pachinko phenomenon in Japan. All the Allied countries were entitled to concessions from defeated Japan. Russia, for example, in addition to the return of Sakhalin to the USSR, was granted the occupation of the four Northern Islands belonging to Japan.

Koreans residing in Japan were given a concession for operating pachinko shops; a lucrative SAC-sanctioned exemption from Japan's list of prohibited gambling activities. An absolute majority of pachinko shops were owned and managed by Koreans, generating enormous revenue.[4] Some of my neighbors and friends were engaged in the pachinko industry. Once when I visited Terada (my birth place) in 1960, our old neighbor was operating a pachinko shop, and behind the shop, a lady was using cash to buy back reward commodities a customer had won playing the slot machine. Her older brother, Mr. Yoon Tonge, whom I saw there after some twenty years, had a much bigger operation in Hiraoka in Osaka.

After the War, pachinko became very popular nationwide and housewives on their way to grocery shopping would spend a little time away from their hectic routines, gambling for entertainment and relaxation, frequently with some reward.

The pachinko gaming industry is unique in its history and background—a fascinating sociological phenomenon in Japanese culture. It invites valuable research in the economics of hospitality, with implications for the much-debated advent of IR (Integrated Resorts) in Japan.

4. Reported by Fortune in 2017, Japan's pachinko market generates more gambling revenue than that of Las Vegas, Macau, and Singapore combined.

2

FROM ABSOLUTE POVERTY TO A FIRST-CLASS AMERICAN EDUCATION

More than half of my life overlapped with the most turbulent period of the twentieth century, and at the doorstep of the twenty-first, I felt a fresh sense of challenge. I experienced both World War II and the Korean War, directly or indirectly. Additionally, I witnessed a series of sweeping historical changes in the United States, Europe, Asia, and all over the world, not just in Korea, including the recent (1997) Asian financial crisis.

There is an American saying: "Don't forecast weather from the window of your home."

The implication of this statement is that one cannot gauge the broader trend from a local vista, but can achieve a higher and wider perspective by leaving one's home and/or country. This doesn't mean one should ignore the importance of the current situation and circumstance, but in my experience, I was able to draw a more accurate and sound conclusion by judging my homeland from a distance.

Even though I spent many years abroad, I never neglected to keep up with Korea. My heart never left the country. While I left my "home window" with the determination to attain a broader and objective perspective of all the changes and developments in Korea from a regional and international perspective, my eyes and ears never left the Korean Peninsula.

History and civilization inexorably proceed, and the world and countries only change. This does not mean, however, that changes in history are random. According to the philosopher Lao-tzu, there are two underlying forces of change in history. One is a centrifugal force that expands outward and pushes toward division and the other is a centripetal force that pulls inward toward union and cohesion. Because of these two opposing forces, the rhythm of history is evolving and macro trends are being formed.

As a student at George Washington University (circa 1959)

International conference, George Washington University years (September 1959)

In some ways, I can say my own life fits this pattern of process. Cultivating myself for standing rightfully as a scholar and an academic required some centrifugal force. I was born the son of a poor farmer family, but managed to go abroad to study and receive a doctorate in the United States. In those days in the 1960s, when even US-educated degree holders were rare, I could have led a comfortable life with my American PhD alone. I chose not to walk on a comfortable career path.

I have always tried to survive and live with good judgment. Being poor, I left home at a young age and pursued my studies without any financial support from my family. I had to work to earn my education. Day in and day out I devoted myself to my studies, ultimately leading me to earn my master's degree from George Washington University and master's and doctoral degrees from the University of Chicago. Benefited by my research achievements and publications, I was able to obtain a Doctorate in Demography from Tokyo University and PhD in Economics from Keio University in Japan.

Not all of my work derived from the desire for academic recognition. I believed there must be a centrifugal force corresponding to a strong centripetal force. In other words, I had a strong belief in connecting my foreign experiences and achievements to my roots in Korea.

The idea behind the Tuman River Development Project and the mission of the Northeast Asia Economic Forum (namely to promote economic integration in Northeast Asia, including Korea), stems from my youthful vision, couched in Lao-tzu's two forces: centrifugal and centripetal. I ultimately became a person who could contribute not only to my own country but also to the Northeast Asia region.

The path of learning and dedicated work abroad can be lost in the whirlpool of the centrifugal force, but the vivid memory of my embarrassing chore as the only boy in a poor Korean village, waking up at frosty dawn to collect the dog's dung on the road for manure, awakened my inherent centripetal force (more on this in chapter 4).

Though I worked in foreign countries for nearly 40 years, the centripetal force propelling me back toward my roots was acting strongly in tandem with the opposing centrifugal force. As time went by, my willingness to contribute to Korea and its people grew stronger. I worried that our values in Korea were falling apart with the introduction of Western culture and technology. However, culture precedes ideology, so no matter how much one tries to uproot it, one cannot.

The failure of the Chinese Cultural Revolution is a good example of this. Culture can be modified, but eradication is impossible. Fortunately, Korean culture is rich, and this is why we should start the twenty-first century with the reflection of the past, one as painful as cutting bones, and remember that we need to be hopeful and optimistic.

3

"SONG OF FLEA"

I was born in Kyoto, Japan in 1936, nine years before Korea was liberated from the Japanese occupation. My parents, who were from Bopsu-myeon, Haman-gun, Gyeongnam, relocated to Japan in the 1920s. We managed to establish a living there thanks to my father, who ran a small workshop making thumbtacks from worn out phonograph records. I had a comfortable childhood. While attending elementary school in Japan, I remember that I was proud of myself as a Korean when I was praised by the Japanese teacher for reciting multiplication tables and doing arithmetic faster than the Japanese children in the class.

My siblings and I did not find living in Japan inconvenient or uncomfortable. My mother took care of her mother-in-law well, which was hard in a foreign country. My grandmother, however, was very unhappy with the Japanese way of coping with the cold weather and frequent earthquakes, and she yearned to return to Korea, a homeland of "warm ondol[1] rooms and no earthquakes," as soon as possible. After the end of the Pacific War in August 1945, knowing my grandmother's strong wishes, my father decided to send her back to Korea before anyone else in the family.

1. In traditional Korean architecture, ondol rooms have underfloor heating that uses direct heat transfer from wood smoke to heat the underside of a thick masonry floor.

With my Japanese neighbor from childhood and my son, Ray (1980)

Even though I was only nine years old and the third child in the family, my father entrusted me with the responsibility of accompanying my grandmother back to Korea ahead of the other family members. He believed that I would be able to safely handle his mother's return even at a young age.

I had no idea as a child what lay ahead of us. I was excited to go along with my grandmother. The reality of a trip to Korea, in a few words, was an enormous change for me, a boy used to living a comfortable life in Japan. While crossing the Japan Sea from Maizuru on a ship, waves as big as a hill hit our boat and I was seasick and terrified.

Arriving at Busan Station, we tried to board a train. In the midst of a crowd of passengers trying to get on board, we barely got on the train. The bustling crowd at Busan station, as people flocked to return to their hometowns, reminded me of bean sprouts sprouting in a pot.

To avoid missing the train on an ad hoc schedule in the chaotic crowd, we pushed and pulled and I saw one person with something like a crowbar intentionally break the window to get on to the train. It was totally lawless.

Concerning this post-war chaos in Korea, a friend of mine of the same age, Hur Sam Soo, told me years later about the following experience he himself had at the Busan Port around the same time, coming ashore from an evacuation ship from Japan. At the pier, Hur's family was spread around with their belongings, waiting to finish the procedures for getting on the train to their hometown, Sanchong, further west. He felt odd when his mother constantly warned him to watch their belongings to protect them against snatching by the "Goat Keeper," since he, like me, was used to a more orderly situation with fewer burglaries in Japan, even after the War.[2]

The chaos and civil disobedience at Busan were manifestations of the transition from Japanese colonial rule to liberation and democracy. The populace, a good majority being illiterate, was far from understanding the true meaning of freedom and democracy—based on civic society and informed by the rule of law and individual obligations. Using the catchphrase of "freedom" at the time and riding on anti-Japanese sentiment, many Koreans exhibited sabotage behaviors unbecoming of a free and democratic society, such as breaking a train window to get on the train, tearing the soft seat covers from the train because "it is a Japanese train," exhibiting chaotic behavior instead of *narabi* (queuing in line in Japanese) for any service.

With many years in the military, my childhood friend Hur Sam Soo, would grow up to play a crucial role in launching the Fifth Republic of Korea, headed by President Chun Doo Hwan in 1980, serving as one of his key confidants.

2. The "Goat Keeper" is a mythical being, akin to the boogeyman, meant to scare children into behaving properly.

As a general, Hur initiated controversial social programs intended to reeducate undesirables such as gangsters and dope traffickers.

According to my friend General Chang Suk Kyu, who played a central role in the overall planning and monitoring of military and state affairs under the direction of President Chun and his close assistants, these programs had their precedents in the initial stage of Park Chung Hee's military revolution of May 16, 1961. Immediately after the May 16 coup d'état, Colonel Park Chang Ahm, a close associate of Park Chung Hee formerly of the North Korean Army, came to the Korean Military Academy to clarify for the cadets that the objective of the revolution was not a communist movement, but an uprising aimed at national reconstruction based on social justice. General Chang Suk Kyu played a central role in overall planning and monitoring military and state affairs under the direction of President Chun and his close assistants, including General Hur Sam Soo.

General Sam Soo Hur in Japan (1984)

General Suk Kyu Chang on the left, Ambassador Richard Walker (second to the left) in Honolulu (circa 1990s)

In Japan, when he was a visiting fellow at Kyoto University, General Hur and I travelled together to Tokuyama in the west and saw the protective hole his father had dug to escape during the American bombings. After sharing our similar experience in Busan, he told me that his initiative for social purification came from his childhood experience at Busan Port and in Tokuyama. On the basis of our interactions with those who were raised in Korea, we agreed that socialization and childhood education can play a crucial part in one's outlook toward society and human relations. Hur mentioned that he had some difficulty working with President Chun, who was raised in Manchuria, China, particularly concerning the issue of rule abidance.

On May 18, 1961, two days after the uprising, General Chang, as a third-year cadet, participated in a parade in the center of Seoul in support of Park Chung Hee and his revolution. Shortly afterwards, the so-called social undesirables, such as mafia leaders, hoodlums, drug traffickers, corrupt salon operators, and others were rounded up and forcefully paraded holding signs of repentance on the same streets of Seoul. A couple of the most notorious gang leaders were sentenced to death.

My 68-year-old grandmother and I, a nine-year-old boy at the time, finally finished the rough hour-long train ride and arrived at Kaya station. From there, we walked 20 kilometers to our final destination. After a long journey across the ocean of Japan, a crowded train, and a seemingly endless walk by road, we finally reached the remote village of our ancestral home.

More adversity awaited us. The living conditions and quality of life were far inferior to Japan. There was not sufficient food to eat. I really didn't understand why my grandmother missed her hometown so much. It was a mystery to me as a young child that she was so relaxed and satisfied in a tiny dark room in a small, old, thatched house.

With the arrival of my parents and siblings, our family together faced a new life reality in Korea. In Japan, we maintained a comfortable standard of living. In Korea, we were confronted with extreme poverty bordering on starvation, and my parents were not able to provide adequate daily meals.

It was heartbreaking and painful for my parents to see us in such dire circumstances. There also was a post-war cholera epidemic killing many people, and during the first year, due to the painful scarcity of food, we ate the husks of beans from which oil had been extracted in Manchuria and then distributed to the villagers. We mixed this ugly industrial material with vegetables to make gruel for our meals and all suffered from diarrhea.

Additionally, there was a high prevalence of scabies in the villages. Our raggedy clothes and seldom-washed underwear in the winter were easily infested with lice, making all of us itchy and irritated. Occasionally in the evening some of us sat around the flickering *horong* (a small kerosene lamp similar to a lighted candle) holding our underwear near the light to locate and kill the lice. When we found a line of lice eggs, we would place them in the heat of the lamp to hear a gratifying "tatatata" sound, like that of roasting sesame seeds.

This fondly reminds me of Beethoven's "Song of Flea," which was written in a Vienna infested with fleas.[3] There is a Korean adverb *ijapdeshi*, with a meaning akin to catching lice, that is used when reading a book or report to mean "thoroughly, without missing a word."

My younger brother Muno, a twin, was a handsome and lively boy of four. He died, leaving his twin sister Munja alone. She was also sick but survived, probably because of the gender advantage in childhood mortality.

The money my father earned in Japan and sent to Korea turned out to be useless during the postwar turmoil in the remote countryside of Korea. Faced with this abrupt circumstantial change, along with my family, I had to battle with poverty, but I never gave up having a dream. As the years passed, I frequently thought that poverty and hardship at that young age ultimately had a positive influence on my subsequent development.

---

3. This satiric song, Ludwig van Beethoven's op. 75, no. 3, is his arrangement of the poem "Flohlied" from *Faust* by Johann Wolfgang Goethe. The reference seems to be a personal interpretation of history.

4

HARD LESSONS IN RESPONSIBILITY, HONESTY, AND PATIENCE

Upon moving from Japan to our village in Korea, my whole family had the challenge of overcoming hunger and poverty. Everyone, including the younger ones like myself, were mobilized to increase the productivity of a few small lots of farmland under our cultivation.

One of my assigned chores was to wake up at dawn and pick up the dog's dung on the road. Dog feces were mixed with straws in a puddle and used as manure. This was the sort of work that was normally done by older men. I felt quite embarrassed since I was the only one among the kids in my village who was doing this dirty work.

The smell of the waste was awful and I hated waking up early in the morning when most kids were sleeping. It was particularly difficult in the winter when the nights were long and cold. When the weather was freezing, the droppings froze and hardened, and the dung didn't smell as bad and it was much easier to collect it. On warm rainy days, the situation was the opposite. My chore was hard and miserable. The smell was unbearable and the soft droppings were very messy and difficult to collect. Many times, I wanted to hurry and quit before the collection was half finished. However, it was not

Golfing at Waialae Country Club, Hawai'i (circa 2000s)

possible to cheat my father. The amount of the feces I picked up every morning was inspected by my father for his approval of my performance before he personally emptied the "dog litter bag" into the manure pit.

Even now, during this time of the coronavirus, when the Waialae Country Club Golf course opened in Honolulu and one could walk with a push cart or while carrying a golf bag, my first thought after I placed the strap of my bag on my right shoulder was that the way I carried it and the weight of the bag was roughly the same as that of the "dog litter bag."

The contrasting difference in this milieu is like purgatory and paradise: in the former, one looks for the most repulsive dung during the sweet morning hours of childhood sleep and in the latter, one looks for a clean white golf ball on the shining green fairway or in the rough grass, under a blue sky with white clouds in the comfortable afternoon temperature. My nine-hole walks invigorated me with the memory of the rice-straw bag, but now they were combined with the sights and sounds of paradise. I enjoyed imagining the origin of the golf game going back to the time of a shepherd with a stick herding lamb in the hills of the Scottish countryside, with the contrasting picture of a poor Korean boy traversing his village collecting dog feces; both in a common pursuit of productivity in agriculture and animal husbandry.

After my morning chores, I walked six to seven kilometers to Jeonggok Elementary School. On the way, I took a little boat that crossed the Nam River at a place called Hominaru, and then walked three to four kilometers to Junggyo where my elementary school was located. Going to school was very difficult. During the rainy season, the river overflowed for over a week, so there were times when I was absent from school for that period. When the weather was cold and windy, the boatman didn't show up at all, so I had to return home. It was difficult to catch up with schoolwork when I missed school for more than a week. After attending the third and fourth grade at Jeonggok Elementary School, I transferred to Kwandong Elementary School. The distance to school was somewhat longer, but the absences caused by the river situation disappeared.

Nevertheless, my father told me to go to school every other day. He felt short of hands with the family farm work and believed all of his children had to stay home and work. During this time, the nickname *haru-ppacom* was attached to me. *Haru* ("day" in Korean, but also meaning "present") was signified with an "O" and *ppacom* ("absent" in Korean) was signified with an "X" in my school attendance record, so *haru ppacom* roughly translated to "every other day hole" in Gyeongsang satoori, or dialect.

In spite of my frequent absences, I was selected to represent the school in a regional drawing competition participated in by all the elementary schools in the region. It took place in the city of Jinju, an educational center of the province, quite a distance away. I was delighted because I could get away from farm work and see a lively city. I hadn't been to an urban scene since leaving Japan. My parents were pleased that I was recognized as the best painter in my school. Before my departure, they heated a bucket of water in the kitchen and gave me a quick wash, a rare occasion, since there were no bathing facilities in the village. In the summer, we could wash ourselves in the river.

I walked about eight kilometers to my teacher's house for an overnight stay and the next morning, we walked to Gunbuk station to catch a westbound train to Jinju, at that time a terminal for all the trains from Busan and Masan. In Jinju my teacher, Mr. Kim Mun Ho, along with another colleague of his, treated me with "Jinju *bibimbap*" for lunch (well known for its taste.) For me, it was out of this world. I didn't win anything, but I was proud to represent a poor remote village school at the time.

In a span of three years, I thoroughly experienced the hard life of a poor village. From this experience and hardship, I learned a valuable and indelible lesson. Whatever is assigned and entrusted to me, I need to finish, no matter what. Deceiving and lying to others does not work. If you have set a destination and goal, even if you have to walk all the way to the end, you need to have the patience and perseverance to walk the distance and attain the goal. I feel my determination and patience in the process strengthened me.

Because of my hard-earned lessons and values, I do not tolerate those who lie and deceive. Nor do I accept a society where lies and deception work. Having been abroad for a long time, it is deplorable for me to see that lies prevail more in our Korean society than in other country.

In order to progress toward and develop into a society based on trust, we need not only formal education focused on knowledge content, but also "human education" combined with the inculcation of right values at school and home.

The right kind of education required in a society based on trust must turn away from the (university) entrance examination–oriented education focused on cramming and turn to a more "human education" consonant with a civic society based on trust. This should start from elementary school. I understand in England, education and training with an emphasis on honesty continues during all six years of elementary school.

Can a true leader emerge in a society where lying is not considered a serious offense? We should not take lightly the age-old lesson and wisdom of Asia that a "Nation without trust will ultimately perish" (無信之國終必滅).

5

ANY FOOD IS ACCEPTED AS PRECIOUS AND VALUABLE

Understanding the precious value of any kind of food is a gift I acquired from my childhood poverty. Lunch during my school years was usually 100 percent barley or sweet potato with kimchi. Some days I had to skip lunch, and on the way back home, I chewed arrowroot to ease my hunger.

Horticulture middle school years (circa 1948–1950)

In winter, things in our village were worse. Food was even more scarce. Instead of barley, we had barley porridge mixed with dried sweet potato stems and leaves. My father, who was trying to feed his family at any cost, bundled and dried a lot of sweet potato stalks and leaves on the outer wall of our thatched house before the winter. When dried, they were mixed with a small amount of barley to make porridge. This way our big family of ten could at least avoid starvation. My father made a desperate effort to get the whole family, bordering on starvation, out of poverty as soon as possible. It's ironic that the food I ate during that time is considered super healthy food now.

My lunch was either 100 percent barley without a single grain of white rice, or sweet potatoes. Some days my mother couldn't pack either for me. I ate so much barley and sweet potato as a child that I do not really enjoy eating those foods anymore. I eat them purely for health reasons now.

My older sister helped the family prepare meals. She expressed to me later that it was heartbreaking and painful not to be able to give extra food to her younger brothers and sisters when they were screaming for more. When I see children who are well fed these days, I feel happy for them, but at the same time they remind me of the days when I was so hungry. If I had eaten as well as children today while I was growing up, I might have grown taller than I am now.

Later on, my mother would comment, when seeing me eat healthy food like bran or barley instead of white rice: "You studied so hard to eat well and now that you can afford all kinds of good food, you are going back to the foods you used to eat when we were so poor?"

When one walks around a big city in a developed country like the United States, one often sees people walking their dogs. Everyone carries a plastic bag to clean up the droppings of their dogs. Looking back on my childhood days of collecting dog droppings, I see a stark contrast between my

With my mother, who had eleven children (seven survived, circa late 1970s)

early childhood and these dog owners. Now, the people who clean dog waste aren't poor people, rather they can afford the luxury of feeding and caring for a pet.

As the years go by, my childhood memory of doing dirty chores—of a little boy carrying a hoe and a straw container with shoulder straps in a remote countryside—seems to me like a beautiful image in an East Asian painting. When I see village houses while jogging in Japan, I frequently see sweet potato stems and radish leaves hanging outside the houses or scattered in the yard and I am pleasantly amazed to consider that what I had to eat to survive during my childhood is now a rather expensive, and sought-after food in the world's economically advanced countries. And I feel grateful for having eaten some healthy foods to overcome starvation. I now strongly feel and sense that the world is constantly changing and things turn around and around.

It is a pity to see the people of our country, who have only escaped poverty in a couple of decades, waste food, not recognizing its preciousness and value. The United States is a prosperous country and still carries a Puritan spirit and Protestant ethic. Our country emphasizes frugality, socially and at home. The phrase "clean your plate" is symbolic of this. In Japan, one is also scolded for wasting food. Material deficiency brings about a heart to value what is essential for life. Thanks to the days when I didn't get enough to eat, I basically have no dislike for any food and enjoy almost all kinds of food. It is a gift that poverty gave me.

6

A DARING RUNAWAY

The Kwandong Elementary School had a small number of students and not enough teachers. With some special consideration from the school, I was able to complete the fifth and sixth grade courses in one year. After graduating from elementary school, I felt the strong desire to continue on to middle school. However, my situation at home was not so accommodating.

One day when my father was on an extended trip, I took courage to beseech my mother, who was working in the field, to send me to middle school. My mother said, "How can you leave all the farm work and go on to studying?" and quietly passed me the hoe. It might have been too much to expect a positive reaction knowing that my mother was constantly fighting with overwhelming poverty and work. Nevertheless, I couldn't give up the hope of going to middle school.

That evening, when I finished the day's work still wrapped in disappointment, my older brother approached me quietly. He said that he too wanted to study, but as the eldest son, he could in no way abandon all the family farm work. He told me, "Leave all the responsibilities to me and go to Busan to study," and he placed in my hand a one-way train fare to Busan.

The next day, I woke up before the roosters crowed and set out walking away from home with a bundle of garlic (considered a cash crop) on my back. I walked 20 kilometers to Kaya, the train station where my grandmother and I had arrived a few years before. From there, I took a train to Busan passing through Masan and got off at Busanchin Station, one station north of the Terminal Busan Station where I had pushed and shoved to get on the same train with my grandmother after disembarking from the ship from Japan.

I saw a wide bustling street with streetcars, carriages pulled by horses, ox wagons, and many pedestrians. I hurried to the streetcar stop to go north to Seomyeon where I could switch to another train to Dongnae. Soon afterward, a streetcar packed with passengers stopped and the side door opened, but only a few people stepped off. I pushed myself into the crowded streetcar, but the car door wouldn't close because the large bundle of garlic on my back was stuck and obstructing the door. The street car began moving while the passengers in front of me yanked me and my back bundle safely into the car. It was truly a stressful moment.

It was around sunset when I transferred to the local electric train from Seomyeon to Dongnae to finally arrive where my aunt (my mother's older sister) lived. Holding a piece of paper with my aunt's address, I guessed I was getting close to her house. I noticed a girl a little younger than myself and asked her, "Where's Mr. Kim Kyo-ju's house?" She responded that it was her home and Kim Kyo-ju was her father. This was the first time I met my cousin Buho and we didn't recognize each other at all. Words could not express how happy I was to reach my aunt's house safely after such a tortuous journey.

My fear of having to sleep on the road vanished when my kind-hearted aunt and the whole family warmly welcomed me and my day as a stressful runaway came to a restful end. Having starved all day, I can never forget the delicious hot dinner that followed.

Sophomore in High School (circa 1951–1953)

Looking back, I can't imagine how I dared to venture on that first faraway journey at the age of 12. As I see children these days transported in automobiles even a stone's throw of a distance (as Koreans say "nose diving distance") to schools and other places, I feel that the convenience of their commute to school by car is excessive. Although I cannot make a unilateral generalization, there are times when I doubt whether children entering middle or high school or university are truly driven by their love for learning.

Paradoxically, thanks to my parents, who were unable to afford to send their children to school because of poverty, I acquired a stronger passion and love for learning than anyone else. Over time, my gratitude toward my older brother, who passed away in his early twenties, grows deeper. His personal sacrifice to enable my dream kindled further my passion for study. There is a Chinese maxim (有志竟成), "Where there is a will, there is a way," and this maxim somehow coincides with my experience, and I want to encourage the younger generation to have a great vision and aspiration.

7

THREE MEALS A DAY AND A SCHOLARSHIP

After that long, daring journey, and voraciously filling myself with delicious rice and side dishes, I explained to my extended family how and why I came to be at my uncle's house. When they heard my decision to take the junior high school entrance exam, my uncle shook his head as if he could not believe what he heard. He said, "You just finished the six-year elementary school course in the remote countryside in five years. How can you dare to take the middle school entrance exam?" Still, I insisted on taking the test.

My uncle reluctantly asked me to apply to a vocational school called Busan Horticultural Middle School instead of the reputable Dongnae Middle School, which he said was not only very difficult to enter but also more expensive. He added that even the Horticultural Middle School would not be easy for me. Since I showed such a strong desire to go to middle school, he allowed me to at least take the entrance exam. Even if I passed, the tuition was not cheap, so he was not sure whether I would be able to attend. My mind was completely focused on attending Dongnae Middle School, but I had no choice but to accept my uncle's suggestion. My staying with them was an additional burden to my uncle's family and I couldn't help but choose a school where the tuition was less expensive.

On the day of the announcement of the results of the entrance exam, I went to school alone. There I saw my name written in Chinese characters clearly on the list hanging across the wall of the school ground. I had passed. When I delivered the news to my aunt and uncle, they were genuinely surprised. Although I was not able to attend school every day during my elementary school years, I was very happy to realize my dream of entering middle school. It wasn't the school I wanted, but I was still glad that I could attend an intermediate school.

After enrolling, I studied hard. The required gardening work (practical training) I performed was never inferior to me since I had done so much practical farm work in the countryside. What's more, I was happy I was able to eat three meals a day and attend school every day. After the first semester, I became first in the class, and a year later I was able to achieve first place in the whole school and received the Yeongnam Scholarship. Thereafter, tuition fees were completely waived.

Busan Horticultural Middle School was an agricultural school founded by Dr. Jangchoon Woo, who developed a seedless watermelon (more on this to follow). I was shy and embarrassed that I was going to that school (then referred to as "dung bucket" school because of its use of night soil for fertilizer), but later I found out it was a very good school.

It is a pity that such horticultural schools have disappeared in Korea. There were a number of brilliant teachers at this school who surpassed teachers in any other school. For example, Lee Bok-Kyu, a retired professor at Busan National University, was one of them. He was admitted to the prestigious 3rd High School (Sanko) in Kyoto, Japan. Historically only one person was admitted to this school from all of Korea. Bok-Kyu then went on to the Law School of the University of Tokyo but was not able to complete his law degree due to the ending of WWII. Since he did not have the normal school qualifications to teach at the regular public secondary schools, he was recruited by a far-sighted principal of our school, Kim Heungsoo.

The English grammar I learned from Professor Lee helped me in many ways later in life. Another brilliant mind was our teacher of agriculture and forestry, Mr. Hyun Gyutaek, a graduate of Kenkoku University at the Manchukuo capital, Shinkkyo (now Changchun). He later became the dean of the college of agriculture at Konkuk University in Seoul. Besides his lectures on agriculture, he taught by way of human education the Confucian lesson of "five man," namely: "A man is not a man and if a man does not behave like a man, he is not a man."

There also was an old traditional-style teacher of Chinese characters, Mr. Lee, who, in Korean traditional costume, taught us Chinese character poems by a historically famous and popular Korean poet Kim Ip (Sakkat). Sakkat was very creative in composing verses that satirically expressed social and personal discontent as well as the vulgar side of human beings. I can still recite a couple of Kim Sakkat poems like "*A bowl of rice gruel on the square pine tree table*"—a satirical verse in appreciation for being treated with a meager bowl of thin gruel on a hungry day of a journey. Sakkat definitely prompted my interest in pursuing the study of Chinese characters that led in later years to my indulgence in Chinese classical poetry and literature.

Looking back, when I was engaged only in study (on a scholarship), it was the happiest time of my childhood. It was especially satisfying to me that I could eat rice three times, every day, without skipping a meal. It may seem like an old-fashioned way of thinking, but I am astonished to see children who are fully supported by their parents not only with tuition, but also allowances. It is unbelievable to me to see many of them make poor life choices during their school years, not realizing how fortunate they are. They take the provision of education and affluence of food for granted and

With high school classmates (circa 1952)

show no appreciation. This younger generation is irritated when their parents talk about the difficulties experienced in the old days. I feel heavily compelled sometimes to find a way to offer a wake-up call to the new generation's mindset and their ignorance of the fortune of having plentiful food and educational opportunities handed to them.

In the 1980s I was congratulated heartily by none other than Professor Hayashi, President of Tottori Agricultural University, a university that conducted pioneering work on developing the Japanese "20th Century Pear" known nationally for its refreshing taste. In our first planning meeting for the 1999 Annual Conference of the Northeast Asia Economic Forum in Yonago, Tottori, in the presence of Governor Nishio of Tottori Prefecture, I was introduced to Dr. Hayashi. When I asked him about the "20th Century Pear" and its origin in Tottori, he said he was a graduate of the Agricultural Division of Kyoto University, which is the top school in science, having produced more Nobel Prize winners than any other institution in Japan.

Hayashi was also a student of Dr. Woo Jangchoon, who, in addition to seedless watermelon, revolutionized the Hakusai cabbage eaten today and the Vasunia flower. I told Hayashi I was a graduate of Busan Horticultural School and that President Syngman Rhee, the President of the Republic of Korea, had requested Dr. Woo, as a Korean descendant, to serve his fatherland in his remaining years in the Horticultural Experimental Center connected with the Horticultural School in Busan. I felt at that time it was a felicitous irony. Having been embarrassed for attending "dung bucket school" as a young boy, my horticultural education was later glorified by a leading expert in agriculture.

In recent years it was interesting to find out that Mr. Inamori, founder of the Japanese firm Kyocera in Kyoto and a major figure in business who also served as interim CEO and Chairman of Japan Airlines, restructuring JAL when it was in trouble, is the son-in-law of Dr. Woo, having married his daughter.

8

ENTERING PYONGYANG

When the Korean War broke out in 1950, I was mobilized (as a young student) as a translator. The US military unit was in dire need of someone who could read maps and translate geographical locations from Korean into English. We crossed the Nakdong River, and witnessing the horrors of the war, proceeded to Seoul. We then went on until we crossed the Daedong River into North Korea.

On June 25, 1950, North Korea, armed with Soviet tanks and weapons, crossed the 38th parallel and invaded South Korea, turning the Korean Peninsula instantly into a war zone. For civilians, all social and economic activities of the country were seemingly suspended. Schools and education were no exception.

This was at the beginning of our summer vacation and my cousins from Busan joined us in our hometown village. Only a few days later they returned to Busan on account of the shocking news of the rapid advancement of the North Korean Armed Forces. In less than a month the war came close to our area and we began seeing American jet fighters strafing the hills across the Nakdong River. We were told to evacuate our village for Kaya immediately and then to where we didn't know. Our family packed whatever was valuable and essential in an ox cart and, with our close relatives and friends, moved to Kaya.

We temporarily received shelter with Mr. Yoon's family, our neighbor in Terada, Japan. During a couple days' stay there, my older brother, BokJay, who was six years older than me, was shot in his upper leg by a policeman who asked for his identification card (dominjeung). My brother was slow to get his ID from deep inside the right-side pocket of his loose Korean style trousers and was suspected of trying to conceal a weapon like a pistol. Today this would likely be considered police brutality.

I had been told that as a child of three or four years in Japan, BokJay was taken to the Nara Zoo after WWII by the neighbors' boys, including Mr. Yoon Dong Kye, a pachinko shop owner. He had stuck his head too close to the fence to see a monkey inside and the monkey had scratched his head, causing both physical and psychological damage. I remember his large scars and all of us in the family noticed the slower physical movements and mental alertness he suffered as a result.

Subsequently, we were told to move east where some freight box cars would be available to transport refugees to an unknown eastern destination, as US and Korean forces were unable to hold the defense line in Haman. I understand the US forces suffered some of the war's heaviest casualties (somewhere in the thousands) in order to hold the last line of defense in the Busan Perimeter on the outskirts of Masan. This was only about 15 kilometers east of Kaya, and reversed a long string of North Korean victories.

Having abandoned most of our valuable baggage, including our treasured ox, all of us, together with relatives and friends, barely got on the last box car out of Kaya. The train moved slowly, pulled by a steam engine locomotive, stopping in Masan and then crossing the Nakdong River bridge at Samrangjin. Finally we stopped at Mulgeum station where we were instructed to get off the train. We were then given the location of Ungsan Elementary School, about 12 kilometers over the ridges and mountain. My cousin had to carry my wounded older brother on a Korean A-frame. Everyone carried their given burden. This was a truly painful march for our family. We reached the elementary school and settled on the school grounds as the classrooms were already filled with the refugees who came before us. Since there were no provisions for food, we had to beg around the village and were thankful for whatever we could get. After a couple of days, I left the family at the school and walked about 35 kilometers to Busan.

My brother was always kind-hearted and compassionate and suffered more than any among our siblings. Being the oldest, with only eight years of education in Japan, in addition to the language barrier, turned out to be a serious obstacle to his adaptation and adjustment to the way of life in Korean rural society. He worked like a dog, but was still studious.

About a year before the Korean War, our family arranged his marriage with a woman in Jungyo across the river, where I first went to the elementary school in Korea. This was also the birthplace of Lee Byung Chul, the founder of Samsung. The traditional Korean nuptial arrangement predicates that the wedding ceremony take place first at the bride's home and a year later the marriage is consummated by the bride joining the groom's family and home (shinhaeng). I still remember during my visit to the home of my future sister in-law, I was royally treated for lunch with cold noodles (kooksoo) to which she added sugar, a precious item. In my brother's case, the War and some tragic happenings intervened in the course of this nuptial journey. When my family returned to their home village after suffering the collective pains of refugee life, my brother apparently studied English on his own to pursue the dream of his own profession. With their consent, he moved to Busan.

In the summer of 1951, when I returned from the frontline, I was surprised and pleased to learn from my aunt that my brother was able to find some work with an American military outfit in Suyeong Military Airport near Haeundae. However, I was disheartened to hear that he had been admitted to the local clinic at Daedong Byongwon for an operation. I joined him in a room at an inn after the surgery. No effective antibiotics were available and he suffered extreme thirst because he was under the strict order to refrain from taking any water or liquid. During the night, right outside of the room, a man with a clear voice was peddling Ice Cakes (popsicles made with sweet red beans) and my brother asked me to buy one for him. I will never forget the pain of refusing his last request. He passed away later that night, only a little after a year after being carelessly shot. Thus, the Ice Cake is part of the memorial ritual we do annually for my older brother.

When I went to school following all of these trials as a refugee, the school was turned into a military base and surrounded by barbed wire. Kim Yong-hwan, my math teacher and the homeroom teacher at the time, was living in faculty housing and I visited him to find out what the situation was.

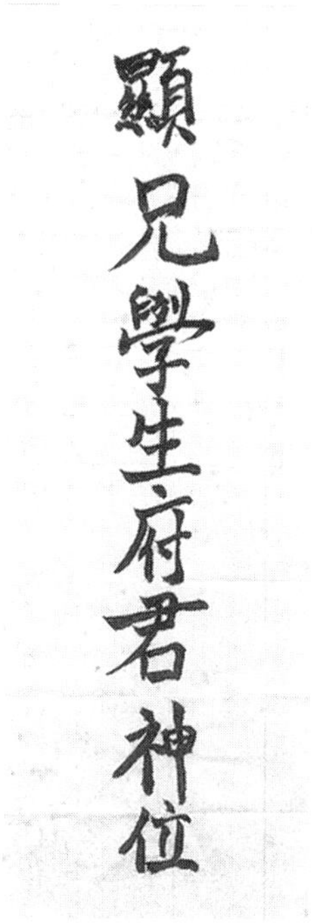

Tablet I wrote in memory of my brother for annual memorial ceremony (*jesa*)

The school had been sequestered by the military for the purpose of reformulating an American artillery unit and normal classes were not possible during that time. I am much indebted to Mr. Kim who understood my predicament and took kind care of me during that difficult period.

On September 15, 1950, under the brilliant command and strategy of General Douglas MacArthur, the U.S. Marines succeeded in an amphibious landing at the port of Incheon and the allied forces moved inland, cutting off the North Korean supply lines and thereby recapturing the capital city of Seoul.

Soon afterwards, the Second Chemical Mortar (4.2-inch) Battalion of the U.S. Army was reorganized at Horticultural Middle School, taking in newly recruited Korean troops. The battalion had about 1000 men and about 300 were Koreans. The Koreans were mostly aged 18 to 40 and recruited on the roadside by the Korean Police and military. They were neither trained nor prepared to fight in the war.

In about a month, this Battalion was about to complete retooling and refurbishing the weapons. The unit needed someone who knew enough English to read the map of South Korea and confirm the locations by name. However, they could not find anyone who could even read "ABC" among the Korean recruits. It was suggested that a student in the Horticultural Middle School who studied basic English would be appropriate. I still don't know who recommended me. It was my homeroom teacher who conveyed to me that I had been mobilized to perform this role when I was only 14 years old.

My unit was commanded by Lt. Col. Edgar Bell and Major Merrit Briggs, second in command. Briggs would succeed Bell in a few months, and it was him to whom I was assigned. I went through the process of getting clearance from Kim Heung-soo, the principal of the horticultural school, and consent from my uncle, my nearest relative. As compensation for mobilizing a minor to join in the combat mission, the battalion delivered three truckloads of the remains of wooden

Fellow student drafted for Korean War with American GI in battlefield (circa 1950–1951)

Korean War zone (circa 1950–1951)

boxes that were used to pack the weapons to my uncle's house. As materials were scarce at the time, those wooden scraps were very useful as timber and firewood. After I was told by my uncle what had taken place on my behalf, I was not without fear of the war, but I decided to take the risk for the venturesome assignment.

Here, an explanation about the English spelling of my Korean name, 조리제 is in order. The surname 조 can be spelled as Jo or Cho as the pronunciation is in between the two sounds "J" and "Ch", and when I used the "Jo" spelling, I was told that it was a girl's name and that Joe was more appropriate. From then on, I was called *Little Joe*, and I used Joe as my surname. I still have old documents with that spelling.

In East Asia, especially in Korea and Japan, one uses an individual's surname followed by *-kun* when addressing a younger person or friend (e.g., *Joe-kun* for me) and *-san* for more collegial relationships. First names are seldom used to address others unless the individuals are very close.

There are several alternative ways of spelling Korean surnames. For example, the first founding President Syngman Rhee of the Republic of Korea, chose *Rhee* for his family name. And President Park Chung Hee, who initially spelled his name *Pak*, was told to consider the spelling *Bag* based on the Ministry of Education's standardization, but he objected, finally choosing *Park*. Years later, Dr. Stuart Rice, in our initial encounter during his first statistical mission visit to Korea (more on this later), told me "Joe" somehow didn't sound right for me and he would like to call me "Joseph," a more sanguine biblical name. Following more common practice, I chose *Cho* as my surname and *Lee-Jay* with a hyphen in the middle to avoid the frequent possibility of confusion with the very common surname *Lee* in Korea and China.

One evening in October 1950, our Battalion moved and Major Briggs, the Executive officer, had Corporal Whiticker as his driver. Whiticker was African American. I sat in the back seat of the jeep and my main task was to check the names of the places wherever we went. I was given a shotgun that could be used to shoot at anything with a rough aim.

After we crossed the Nakdong River and passed through Gimhae, Daegu, and Gimcheon, we were going through a narrow mountain path in Chupungryeong. We heard an exchange of gunshots and encountered what appeared to be the remnants of a North Korean People's Army unit. Our two sides were firing at each other and this was my first combat experience. After the North Korean soldiers were quelled, our battalion again moved north to Daejeon and crossed the Han River. We passed through Seoul and Uijeongbu to reach Sariwon of Hwanghae Province. Rice straw piles were conspicuous all over in the wide plains of the rice fields of Sariwon and the corpses of North Korean soldiers were scattered in the empty rice fields. The tragedy of the war unfolded right before my eyes.

Daedong River Bridge in Pyongyang, North Korea (1992)

When we were crossing the Daedong River to enter Pyongyang, the ROK military police warmly welcomed us at the entrance of the bridge. On both pillars of the bridge I saw the ROK flag held by a dead hand, apparently cut from a North Korean soldier. That horrible scene still vividly remains with me.

9

COMBAT (WITH A DICTIONARY FOR CONSTANT REFERENCE)

In Pyongyang, my assignment was to determine unidentified prisoners, either as our side or the enemy, interpreting with hand and body gestures. This was carried out by grabbing their hair while simultaneously listening carefully to how they spoke, looking for the tone of the dialect. After retreating to the South from the vicinity of the Yalu River, I continued in my role as an interpreter, which was increasingly necessary with the formation of a new ROK Mortar unit. I devoted my time to fully beefing up my limited English by exhausting and wearing out an English dictionary.

After staying in Pyongyang for about a week, our battalion safely moved through Sookcheon, Gaecheon, and Pakchon to safely reach Unsan, noted for its gold mines. This was sixteen kilometers from the Yalu River. In Unsan, we had to engage in fierce battles with North Korean troops. Due to the language barrier and poor communication, the U.S. military experienced many difficulties. At that time, the weather was really cold and lacking a sufficient uniform supply, many of the South Korean soldiers who were new recruits, wore warmly padded and quilted cotton military uniforms taken from the North Korean Army without hesitation. This occasionally led to confusion in differentiating the North Korean soldiers from the South Korean ones. I observed one occasion where our South Korean troops were mistaken for the enemy and the U.S. fighter jets and artillery units bombed and fired at the target, resulting in painful casualties on the part of our troops.

Col. Briggs entrusted me with the task of determining whether unidentified soldiers captured in the vicinity of our Unit's location belonged to the North Korean Army or the ROK Army. The easiest way for me to determine this was to touch and feel the soldiers' heads. If the head was shaved or with short hair, the soldier was North Korean and if the hair was longer, the soldier was with the South Korean army. I could also tell the difference by how the men spoke: listening to their accent and dialects. I had to be extremely careful and accurate in my actions. This identification was truly a suspenseful moment, not only for me in touching their hair but also for the captured soldiers, since their fate, life or death, depended on my judgment.

Towards the end of October and early November of that year, we were unable to advance any further North and had to stay in Unsan. Our Battalion was supporting the ROK 1st Division. Facing an unanticipated massive Chinese attack, the 1st Division broke down and directly exposed our units.

One day, around 2:00–3:00 a.m., our troops were under siege by the Chinese forces. A good part of the 2nd Chemical Mortar Battalion were either killed or captured as prisoners. Our retreat was inevitable. In the cold winter during the freezing hours, it was not easy to start the vehicles. When the engines started after several attempts, those who were mobile got on the vehicles and started the retreat. The Korean troops supported by our mortar unit probably suffered even more casualties.[1]

---

1. "The Red Dragons of the 2nd Chemical Mortar Battalion were never relieved from combat duty. For 1007 consecutive days the battalion . . . 'moved along the entire width of the battleline, emplacing where

A photograph in *Time* magazine on December 11, 1950, portrays a vivid scene of the onslaught of the massive Chinese attack from another angle.

> "Last night about eleven o'clock," said a U.S. major, "My George [G] Company was hit from three sides, the left, right and front, by about three companies of Chinese. One of my patrols picked the first ones up about 150 yards out. The Chinese charged in and overwhelmed us with a real mass attack. About three out of every ten of them were loaded with automatic weapons of some sort—Tommy guns, burp guns or automatic carbines. Others carried .25-caliber Jap rifles. They were all loaded down with grenades."

---

the fighting was heaviest, inflicting tremendous casualties . . . and the rest of [*sic*] redeploying when a relative lull occurred to yet another sector where the savage battle flared anew.'" Thus read one of the battalion's two Presidential Unit citations. The story of this battalion has never been documented. Based on personal interviews and original, long-forgotten and unpublished records, the book *Red Dragons* puts the reader in the trenches on Korean mountainsides in every kind of weather and every kind of action. To the left and right the reader finds soldiers who fought the "Forgotten War" with little reward and by their courage and sacrifice held the line behind which America gathered strength for its ultimate victory in half a century of the Cold War. Author Walter J. Eldredge is a 1968 graduate of MIT and retired from ExxonMobile Corporation. Walt is an experienced backpacker and sailor. He and his wife Peggy live in Baton Rouge, Louisiana, where they are active volunteers with many community organizations and participate in the lives of their five adult children. Walt's father was a mortar company commander with the Red Dragons. Walt says of his work with veterans, "I have shared in the memories of ordinary men who drove themselves to extraordinary limits. I have been able to make those memories available to their families and friends who often have no idea of what these men achieved or what they endured. Many have told me that my work 'broke the ice' for discussions that otherwise would not have taken place. Many of my closest friends are men who fought alongside my father before I was born" (from *Red Dragons: The 2nd Chemical Mortar Battalion in Korea*, by Walter J. Eldredge, Dog Ear Publishing, 2009).

Korean War zone (circa 1950–1951)

Our Battalion barely survived the Chinese onslaught. We managed to withdraw from Unsan, passing through Gaecheon, and finally reaching Seokcheon. During the retreat, as we forded a river away from Unsan, the icy water was rising up to my waist. I was terrified by the fear of drowning. After withdrawing from cold Unsan, we came to Gaecheon, where the Headquarters unit camped by the riverside for one day.

At Gaecheon, there was one unforgettable incident. Late at night, an old Korean man with a young woman who was later identified as his daughter-in-law, appeared before me and told me that the woman had been raped by a soldier. I reported this immediately to Col. Briggs and he instantly assembled and lined up the unit in a fairly spacious yard. He asked the woman and the old man to examine the soldiers' faces, one by one. The commander and I were right behind the two of them. It was very dark and using the flashlight didn't help much in identifying the culprit. After all, Koreans in those days most likely never saw the faces of so many white and black Americans together. After one round, the woman said they all looked alike and she couldn't identify the man who wronged her. As a young boy in combat, I was deeply touched by the moral discipline demonstrated by Col. Briggs and the U.S. military.

The day after, we finally reached a hospital structure in Sukcheon and stayed there for about a week. I spent a good amount of time writing letters for the illiterate Korean soldiers who had also escaped the narrow path of death. The letters were mainly to inform and assure their families and loved ones that they were still alive.

Having suffered greatly in supporting the ROK 1st Division in their failed attempt to hold the line in Unsan, my Battalion felt relieved to be assigned to support American and British Infantry regiments who were much better trained and disciplined. After our stay in Sukcheon, the remainder of the Korean contingent (initially 300 men and somewhat of a burden to the Battalion) was reassigned to ROK units and I was relieved of my duty of writing letters for them.

Our Battalion moved further south to Pyongyang and stayed there for a few days in a nice big house with a piano on which I played some simple school tunes. We then retreated down south to Kaesoung, where we stayed overnight. We met a middle-aged woman (her absent husband was a dentist) with a daughter my age, a schoolgirl named Kim Yong Ja. The next day, the woman and her daughter gave me an embroidered handkerchief with a note containing an address in Seoul, with a Gwanghwamun street and house number. In parting they smiled and said that after the War we would meet each other again in Seoul.

When I went back to Seoul in 1955 for my college education, I looked for the place, since I was looking for lodging and sharing a room with a student from Daegu who practiced his violin every morning. Sadly, I couldn't find any remnants of Kim Yong Ja's house, or her father's dental practice.

Korean War zone (circa 1950–1951)

My battalion then moved rapidly to Yijongbu, Icheon, Daejeon and further down to Gimcheon for an extended period to recoup. We camped out on a hill south of Gimcheon town and I had to improvise off limit signs (like the real estate sale signs of today but in Korean) to prevent intrusion by the local populace.

In Gimcheon, on several occasions, Col. Cooper, along with a couple others, took me along on deer hunting excursions to the mountainous hills northeast of the town. Everybody in the Unit seemed to enjoy deer meat as much as I did for the first time. Refreshed and reorganized, we advanced northward to Icheon and then to Yeoju. From there we went to Gapyeong, where, by a large lake, I saw some dead bodies on the bank that were yet to be disposed of, resulting from a major operation against the Chinese Army. The sounds of the big artillery and salvos of the mortars were deafening. Many years later I heard from an American tank battalion commander (the retired Col. Robert Montague of the 213 Armor Battalion) that at that time the Allied forces were at serious risk of an encirclement by the Chinese Army. He was engaged in that battle and now resides in Hilo, Hawai'i Island.

As the BCB (British Common Brigade) and the 6th ROK Division were retreating, killing hordes of Chinese and at the same time communicating to the Armor Battalion the exact locations where the enemy were concentrated, there was one brave Australian officer who was somehow left behind the enemy lines. According to Col. Montague, tons of artillery shells from 105 howitzers in his tank unit were loosed on those locations to cripple the Chinese attack. For his bravery, and critical actions that turned the tide of the battle, this BCB officer was awarded Britain's highest medal, equivalent to the U.S. Congressional Medal of Honor.

After the Gapyeong engagement, we moved along the North Han River to Hwacheon in the early summer of 1951. At this time the Allied forces were pushing the Chinese Army back inch by inch in fierce fighting and I saw mound after mound of empty shells in the battle zone North of Hwacheon.

In late June, 1951, the Civilian Transport Corps (CTC), a unit of about 600 men, was assigned to the Mortar Battalion to help transport weighty mortars, ammunition and other equipment over the rough terrain and hills north of Hwacheon. They were not well trained and none of them spoke English. This added a logistical burden in managing the Korean unit, but since they brought their own supply of food and auxiliary materials, the Battalion's supply chain was not affected.

The fighting in the front was now deadlocked. Social life in the southern part of Korea showed some signs of stability. In that summer of 1951, shortly after our involvement with the Korean Transport Corporation, I was given a special new assignment for the formation and inauguration of the Korean 4898 4.2-inch mortar unit under the direction of Brigadier General Gilmore, Commander of the 9th Corp of Artillery.

I was given the role of his interpreter. I was really nervous doing translation for the general, but apparently I fulfilled my job well, alongside Major Kim who was constantly at attention. At that time, I was in close interaction with Kim, Commander of 4898th Unit, along with the 8th Cadets of the Korean Military Academy, some of whom treated me like a fun friend. Afterwards, I was curious to hear about Major Kim's whereabouts.

In combat, I learned artillery terms like elevation, deflection, WP ammunition (white phosphor for indicating location), HE shell (high explosive), and so forth. Late in the summer of 1951, there was news that my school was returning to normal classes and I was instructed to return to Busan. Mine was a short military life of ten months, but I carried out the challenging role of bridging the gap between the ROK and the U.S. military with very limited English proficiency, having completed only the second and third grades of middle school. I had to rely heavily on the English dictionary with pages torn and worn out, plus my body language and gestures to communicate.

When I arrived at my aunt's house in the truck that our unit provided, my aunt burst into a loud cry and with tears, hugged me for a long while. They thought that their nephew might have died since they did not hear from me for nearly a year.

Our Battalion Commander offered me a captured Russian-made truck that was taken from the retreating North Korean Army as a kind of reward for my service. I did not know how to drive the truck, nor did I know what to do with it. It was filled with boxes of tobacco taken from an abandoned warehouse in Umsong, Chungbuk, as a token of appreciation.

I witnessed true courage and those who had that courage during my surreal Korean war experience. Courage arises only when one is faced with a crisis and it emerges from a person who calmly responds to a given situation. In contrast, people who talk big often shrink or act cowardly in a crisis.

Years later in the 1980s, under my direction, the East-West Center in Hawai‘i was engaged in numerous cooperative projects with institutions in the People's Republic of China (PRC). Population and economic development were major themes. Along with these projects, we carried out exchanges with high level policy makers and scholars. One fascinatingly serendipitous example was the visit of Mr. Wen Jungyi. He was an ethnic Korean, the former Vice Chairman of State Minority Commission. In the winter of 1950, he was commanding the Korean ethnic corps of the Chinese 8th Road Army that had operated the massive attack on the Allied forces, including the 2nd Mortar Battalion.

When I told him about my combat experience in Unsan, North Korea, and taking the massive frontal attack by his volunteer army, Wen *abai* (senior, in his Korean dialect) was really surprised. I said, “If I had been killed or captured by your soldiers, I might not be here talking with you in Hawai‘i,” and he was stunned but very happy I survived the War. We became acquainted immediately and enjoyed a close friendship until he passed away. I became a mentor to his Chinese son-in-law Wang Dingding, a bright young man who was one of my research assistants. Wang obtained his MA and PhD in Economics at the University of Hawai‘i and lived in Hawai‘i for several years. He is currently teaching at Beijing University, recognized as a leading economist.

During his stay in Hawai‘i, there was an occasion where Mr. Wen Abai was invited to stay at our house for a week with his daughter when we happened to be away. Each time we subsequently saw each other, he would always mention in the presence of others that in my bathroom I kept the Book of Mencius for reading.

Related to this first serendipitous event, there was someone named Roh Kong Kyun, whom I met at the University of Chicago in the 1960s. Roh was studying for an MBA at the Chicago Business School, after having finished his PhD in Economics at Yale University. He later returned to Korea and taught at Seoul National University. Roh wanted to come to the East-West Center as a visiting fellow and I helped him to join the East-West Population Institute. As we were socializing, he wanted to ask me to do him a special favor and I told him I would try to help him. He said it was very personal and strictly confidential.

Kong Kyun was from a well-to-do family who owned a department store in Jinampo in North Korea and his father told him to go south to study at Seoul National University in the uneasy situation before the Korean War broke out. His oldest brother, with a socialist orientation, had moved away from home a number of years earlier and joined the communist revolution in China. Roh came to South Korea and entered SNU, but because of his older brother's situation, he felt very insecure and found a way to go abroad to study, eventually attending Yale University. After the situation changed for the better in Northeast Asia, he knew I was working closely with the PRC and he told me he wanted to locate his older brother in China.

This was just a few months after our mutually fascinating historic encounter with Mr. Wen, resulting in a close friendship. I told Professor Roh that I would try to help him because I knew someone who could help from China. A few days later I asked Mrs. Wang Dingding (Xiao Li) about locating someone: an ethnic Korean in the Korean Chinese community. She asked for the exact name of the person and when I spelled out the name, she instantly recognized the same person who had for years worked closely with her father. We arranged for her to come to our house on a weekend for a telephone conversation with Mr. Wen, her father. During this unforgettable telephone conversation with her father, the dramatic facts were revealed.

Mr. Roh, the older brother of Roh Kong Kyun, received a communist party education including military training to become high cadre and for a number years he worked for Mr. Wen and lived with his family in the neighborhood. He fought in the Korean War as one of Wen's senior staff and was also part of the Chinese force that attacked our unit in North Korea.

I was able to arrange for the two brothers to communicate with each other. Furthermore, the next year it just so happened I had already planned a field trip to Xi'an, to be hosted by Xi'an Jiaotong (Transportation) University for the East-West Population Institute annual summer seminar. The younger brother Kong applied for the field trip and on our way to Xi'an, at the Beijing Airport, after so many intervening years, the two brothers had a dramatic reunion with tears and smiles in their eyes. The younger brother later confided to me that his older brother regretted his career choice of becoming a communist and apologized for the family tribulation he had caused.

10

"NOBLEMAN OPERATOR"

After returning from the war, I returned to the Horticultural School, attending the ninth grade. However, the situation at the school was a little different from the time before I left for the war zone. The scholarship I had received before the war wasn't there and I was concerned I was becoming a burden to my uncle's family. My parents returned safely from their refugee life to the countryside and continued farming, but could not afford to send me tuition and boarding.

After much thought about achieving an independent future, I remembered a letter that I had received from Colonel Ivan Cooper when I was leaving the frontline. He had written a letter of introduction and recommendation for me in case I needed it in Busan. Cooper, a U.S. military lieutenant colonel of the 2nd Chemical Mortar Battalion, referred me to the 68th Smoke Generator Company in Busan where I would work as a telephone operator. This opportunity allowed me to attend the school during the day and work at night, sleepless. Transferring to a better position allowed me to help support my family in the village in Haman.

On Cooper's recommendation, I went to see Captain Pauli at the U.S. military base in Busan, formerly a faculty member at Ohio State University. I asked him whether he could find me a part-time job and shortly afterwards, I received a message in return. I was offered a part-time job as a telephone operator for the 68th U.S. Smoke Generator Company. This work allowed me to go to school during the day and work at night. Working hours were from 7:00 pm to 6:00 am but after 10:00 pm the lines were not so busy, giving me a chance to study. Sometimes I could play a chess game with a young ROTC officer whose small frame and intellectual appearance earned him the nickname "Shrimp Boat."

I recall wanting to doze off after midnight, but I couldn't because I didn't know when the phone would ring. One night, a siren sounded to signal combat readiness and all the lights were turned off at once. The telephone rang and I grabbed the handset in a hurry and shouted "Nobleman Operator" continuously. I could not hear a response. Suddenly, someone entered the room with a flashlight and I saw the duty officer standing in front of me. He said: "Why didn't you answer the phone calls sitting right in front of the switchboard?" I was dumbfounded. I was holding the flashlight in my ear. When I came to my senses, I realized I had mistakenly picked up the L shaped flashlight in the dark and was shouting "Nobleman Operator" (the password) at the flashlight. I had fallen asleep while working in front of the switchboard. The officer on duty burst into laughter and left the room with only a light warning. This was the consequence of my strenuous routine of an excessive workday and night without getting enough sleep.

When I was in the fourth year of middle school (equivalent to 1st year in today's high school), I transferred to Bukbusan Night School, located near the American military camp. My plan was to work full time during the day to increase my income in a better paying position where I could fully use my ability and potential. Eventually I could quit working and concentrate on studying during my senior year in high school. Then, I intended to go to college.

Working as Nobleman Operator at Army Base (1955)

With American GIs and high school classmates (circa 1952–1955)

With the recommendation of my chess friend, a ROTC officer, I was able to land a better job. It was at the U.S. military unit's labor management office, checking the attendance of 150 Korean laborers to calculate their salaries and wages. Thanks to this job, I was able to successfully complete my second year of Bukbusan High School as planned and fully concentrate on study during my third year at the Horticultural School. When my father learned that I was earning a decent income as a student, he made a regular trip to Busan around payday to ask for financial help to contribute to the cost of living for my family in the countryside and to cover the cost of education for my younger siblings. Once, he asked me to invest in buying a calf and I remember doing my best to achieve that goal.

In retrospect, although it was painfully difficult to carry on with my studies and work part-time simultaneously at a young age, it was truly a valuable experience. When Confucius was young, he was said to have been employed in various practical work, such as accounting and carpentry. Suffering is a precious nutrient for life.

Sgt. Robert Parris (center), US Army, of the 68th Chemical Smoke Generator Company in Busan (1955)

11

POVERTY-STRICKEN COLLEGE STUDY

Entering the Hankuk University of Foreign Studies, I majored in English and studied Spanish and German. I had room and board at Haebangchon, then a poor area inhabited mostly by North Korean refugees, and I was desperately earning my way up.

From my third year of high school, I set my goal early for studying in the United States and started to go through the process. Thanks to my experience and connections working with the U.S. military, it was easy to secure the necessary documents, including an affidavit of financial support. The procedure for study abroad was completed smoothly. I thought my plan for studying in the US would come through soon, but I decided to go to college in Korea until I received my visa. I was a bit hesitant because of the higher cost of room and board of living in Seoul but I finally decided to move from Busan to Seoul.

In preparation for my study abroad, I entered Hankuk University of Foreign Studies, a university which was recruiting students through entrance examinations and attracting students from other first-rate schools. Rumors that the university's faculty were excellent and influencing students from top-notch universities to transfer to Hankuk was also a factor in my selecting this university. I applied to the English Department with emphasis on culture and literature and chose Spanish and German as my second and third foreign languages. During the first year at the University, there was an embarrassing occasion where before his lecture, President Ahn Ho Sam asked me to stand up before the class and turn my head. He then said "Look at Student Cho Lee-Jay's head. This is a typical shape of the head of a genius." I felt really awkward in that I was paraded like a chimpanzee on one hand, but complemented on the other. The way I saw it, I barely passed the University entrance examination coming from a provincial agricultural high school. I certainly did not feel I deserved to be paraded in front of my classmates.

Around that time, I anticipated that Japan would rise again through rapid economic revival, and I also wanted to study Japanese, but the Japanese language department had not yet been established. Instead, I ignored the ridicule of others and self-studied Japanese. I asked one of my relatives in Japan for an onerous favor: sending me the Japanese textbooks from first elementary school to the third year of high school, which I diligently used for my Japanese studies.

In addition to languages, I studied statistics, economics, and history. Professor Robert Rainer from Oxford University, England, was teaching at the University and he gave an excellent series of lectures on English literature. Some faculty members of the English literature departments of Seoul National University and Korea University, including Koh Seok Koo and Kang Bong Soo (the latter a graduate of the prestigious Tokyo University) joined us in the lectures. Professor Rainer later moved to Seoul National University, and I am grateful to him for always remembering me and for kindly welcoming me after graduation.

Meanwhile, my plan for going abroad to study did not work out as expected. My passport had been issued, but the visa was not forthcoming. I had to give up my dream of studying in the United States, and instead decided to make the best of my college education in Korea. As my financial situation deteriorated, I did whatever I could to earn income, such as translation and tutoring, in order to continue my studies. At one point, I couldn't bear it and returned to my village in the countryside to rest for a couple of months. In my second year of college, I found a job at a small magazine company specializing in economic statistics, but I quit soon afterwards because I wasn't paid for several months. Nevertheless, I felt I had been compensated in a way by acquiring a basic knowledge of economics and economic statistics as building blocks for my future study and work in the field.

Helping family around the farm (College years in Haman, circa 1955–1957)

College years (circa 1955–1957)

I lodged at Haebangchon "Liberation Village," a poor village at the Southside of Namsan Hill overlooking the Han River. This lodging was introduced to me by my classmate from college, Kim Hyukchun, who was from a refugee family from Jongju, North Korea. The reason was that I wasn't getting enough food at other lodgings. I can't forget the kindness of my host, Prosecutor Im's widow, who fed the boarders, saying in a North Korean dialect, "Eat a lot, eat a lot." "Liberation Village" is now "Buchon," which means rich village, but at the time of my lodging there, the roads were not paved and when it rained in the summer, the hilly narrow paths were muddy. In the winter, when the heavy snow froze the terrain, it was extremely difficult to walk. One winter evening, I was carefully climbing a narrow steep hill covered with frozen snow and at about 30 meters, a young girl in the front suddenly slipped, pushing down four people in front of me and we all slipped together, in order, hitting each other. Six of us piled up at the bottom of the frozen slippery path like a mound. Reflecting on that scene, which was embarrassingly confusing at the time, I can't help but laugh now.

12

AN INTERNATIONAL REPRESENTATIVE OF THE REPUBLIC OF KOREA

Working as a government statistician, I focused on studying statistics. In 1958, the Meeting of Chief Statisticians for Asia and the Pacific was hosted by UNESCAP in Bangkok and I attended as a representative of the Republic of Korea. This was the first time I had ever taken a flight, and for me the meeting provided an opportunity to get acquainted with foreign experts and broaden my view of the world economy.

From 1957, I edited the *Korea Economic Statistics Monthly* in the Ministry for Reconstruction, the predecessor of the Economic Planning Board of Korea. In the early days, the scale of Korea's economy was very small, and so, each month, in order to collect production statistics on industrial outputs, I used a jeep supported by the United Nations Korean Economic Reconstruction Commission (UNCRA) and traveled to relevant Ministries and associations. For example, with bicycle production, only a little over 300 units were assembled each month, and by virtue of this work, I was able to read a good many books and reference materials on economic statistics. This helped greatly for me to build a theoretical basis for my future work. Dr. Maxwell was the statistical advisor to the Ministry of Reconstruction at the time, and I was also the interpreter for his lectures on statistics at the College of Commerce of Seoul National University.

In 1958, the United States dispatched the Rice Statistical Mission aimed at improving Korea's overall statistics as part of its technical assistance to Korea. The head of the mission was Dr. Stuart A. Rice, who was a prominent scholar and successfully undertook the reform of the Japanese statistical system at the request of MacArthur's SAC (Supreme Allied Command) in Japan after World War II. Having taught at the University of Pennsylvania (as a founder of the Sociology and Economics Department), Dartmouth, and the University of Chicago, he was a pioneer of quantitative analysis in the social sciences in the US, and played a leading role in the reorganization and modernization of the U.S. Government's statistical system under President Roosevelt, overseeing its implementation in the Executive Office under President Truman. I was assigned to work with Dr. Rice and his team. The opportunity to work with a world-renowned scholar was a valuable lifetime fortune and blessing to me. I assisted him in his work with all my strength and ability.

Dr. Stuart Rice

Working with Dr. Stuart Rice (circa 1958)

In December of the same year, I attended the 2nd Chief Statisticians Meeting of the United Nations Asia-Pacific Regional Economic and Social Council (ECAFE) in Bangkok, Thailand, as a Korean representative, along with Consul Ji Yun Tae, who later served as an ambassador, representing the Foreign Ministry. It was extremely rare for government officials to go abroad for a meeting, and on every occasion for such a meeting abroad, the request had to be submitted up to the Gyeongmudae (currently, Blue House, Office of the President) for approval by Korea's President. For the first time in my life, the major newspaper, *The Dong-A Ilbo* (daily) reported (with a tiny photo of me) on the front page in November 1958, that I would be participating in this international conference.

My first flight ever was from Seoul (Yeouido Airport) to Tokyo, and after an overnight in Tokyo our delegation flew to Hong Kong where we stayed for two days. There, with a government allowance for attending an international conference, I bought a suit to wear at the conference. It was my first suit, carefully selected for the occasion. On the first day of my stay at the Sariyanon Hotel in Bangkok, I felt quite nervous after several days' journey via Tokyo and Hong Kong (whereas today one can fly directly from Seoul to Bangkok by jet). I was concerned about the instruction from the Ministry of Foreign Affairs that we were allowed to interact only with the delegates from "free countries" such as the United States, the Republic of China, the Philippines, etc., and we should refrain from contacts with representatives of Japan and neutral countries like India.

Bangkok/ECAFE Statistical Conference with Ji Yun Tae (right, 1958)

Meeting in Hong Kong (1958)

In the course of the conference, however, I had conversations with representatives from allies, as well as from India and Japan, on the technical side of census and statistics. Despite warnings from my colleagues from the Foreign Ministry, which I had the courage to ignore, I met and interacted with the representative of India, an elite senior civil servant, Asok Mitra, Registrar General, who later became permanent Secretary overseeing India's economic planning. Personally, we became close enough to exchange joking notes during the meeting. Thanks to this acquaintance, after a number of years, I was able to conduct international research projects related to India.

The representative of Japan was Dr. Minobe Yokichi, Director of Statistical Standards of the Prime Minister's Office, later elected as Governor of Tokyo. He had worked with Dr. Rice during his postwar statistical mission and thanks to Rice's special introduction, we met in Bangkok and have since maintained a close friendship. The technocrats who worked under Dr. Minobe later became prominent figures in government and industry in Japan. Benefiting from the network I developed beginning at that Bangkok meeting, I have continued to engage in numerous cooperative activities with Japan.

After attending the international conference in Bangkok, I felt desperately that Korea was behind other countries in all aspects. My determination to go abroad by all means to receive professional education and training became much stronger. In addition, through the Bangkok conference I was able to gain some confidence in international meetings. It was an enormous personal gain for me to get acquainted with many prominent foreign personalities.

13

SWEATING IT OUT IN WASHINGTON, D.C.

The opportunity to study abroad finally came. In the words of my father, I was knocking at the chance. My frustration over the earlier denial of my study plan was redeemed by my application through a civil service competition and selection for a traineeship at the United States Department of Commerce. Sweating it out through a year in an attic, I was able to complete a Department of Commerce training program and simultaneously, the requirements for a master's degree from George Washington University (attending evening classes). It was the fruit of my lifelong passion for study.

In 1959, the Korean government, in cooperation with the U.S. government, was implementing an overseas technical training program for civil servants using the International Cooperation Administration (ICA) fund. Candidates recommended by each Ministry took the test. Although the competition was intense, I was notified by the Department of the Ministry of Reconstruction that I was selected with the best score.

I was totally elated. Although it was a short training period of one year, the road to study in the United States was wide open again after my earlier plan to study abroad failed. As a member of the Economics and Census training group of the U.S. Department of Commerce, I was allowed to take relevant academic courses at George Washington University in Washington, D.C. I was to be paid a very generous living allowance of $360 per month, and in addition, the tuition for my university courses would be covered.

At the time of my departure, along with other trainees, I was given a first-class flight according to the US's official travel standards. After taking off from Gimpo Airport, in JAL's First Class section, the flight attendants offered various luxurious drinks, including champagne. I thought we were paying for drinks and my colleagues and I declined every time they offered.

When we arrived in Honolulu, we found out that all the drinks were free, so we realized that our behavior had been that of "Korean countrymen." After two days and three nights flying through Tokyo, Honolulu, San Francisco, and Chicago, I finally arrived at Washington National Airport, completing over 30 hours of flying time. At the airport, Dr. and Mrs. Rice warmly welcomed me.

Dr. Rice provided valuable advice for me to make the best use of my precious time of one year in the United States. He also introduced me to important people in academic and research institutions. Firstly, he arranged a lunch occasion for us with Professor Brown, Graduate Dean at George Washington University, and asked whether there was a way for me to start the MA program by taking evening classes. Dean Brown said I could register for courses as a special student prior to formally being accepted to the MA program. If my course grades were good, the school would recognize the credits toward my MA before the completion of my requirement for graduation. Dr. Rice appreciated Professor Brown for his cooperation.

It was really tough to complete twelve required courses in the evening within a year. For me however, it was a rare opportunity to do both the training program and a

George Washington University (September 1959)

master's degree in a year. I attended the Commerce Department training sessions Monday through Friday from 9:00 a.m. to 4:30 p.m., which included lectures and practical exercises on national income analysis and population statistics. The Department of Commerce allowed only two college courses for trainees, so as not to interfere with the day-time training. When I requested tuition support for three courses, the Commerce Department (more specifically the Census Bureau person in charge of training) expressed reluctance, responding that not only would this add to the Department of Commerce's budgetary burden, it would be difficult for a foreigner who had never studied at an American university to do the task. With the help of Dr. Rice, however, I was allowed to continue my training work during the day and study at night. As expected, it was not an easy task.

I always read books or notes related to my studies when I was on the Census Bureau shuttle bus or eating. There were several opportunities for industrial observation tours organized by the Department of Commerce, but I gave up most of them and devoted myself to study. At that time, one of the trainees who joined me in skipping the trips and studying hard was Park Sung-sang, a former governor of the Bank of Korea. The memory of wrestling with books while sweating in attic lodgings during that hot summer without air conditioning became one of our favorite topics whenever we met afterwards.

As originally planned, I was able to complete the U.S. Department of Commerce's training program with honors and at the same time, the requirements for my master's degree at George Washington University.

George Washington University offered me a scholarship to continue my graduate work for a PhD, but I chose to return home to complete my official obligation as a Korean public servant. My return trip to Korea involved getting a transit visa for 14 days, and it provided me with a precious opportunity to return to Japan and see Tokyo for the first time.

As soon as I arrived at Haneda Airport I was able to arrange to buy a ticket to Kyoto on an overnight steam engine express (the fastest at the time). The next morning at Kyoto Station, at track 9, I changed to a local *Naraden* train of yellowish color, a train I recalled from my childhood, to reach Terada, my birth place and destination.

Return visit to Japan (circa 1960s)

In the fifteen years since I had left, the town looked pretty much the same, and I was able to find my way to the location of our old house. In possession of the latest news of a distant relative of ours who resided in the same neighborhood (a close neighbor and family friend, and the younger sister of Yoon Dong Kye) I located my relative, Cho Yong Baek, and his family. They were surprised and glad to see me. I requested Mr. Cho to guide me the next day to my aunt's (my father's oldest sister's) home in Otsu Shiga-ken.

During the night I noticed an enlarged portrait of Kim Il Sung (North Korea's Supreme Leader) on the wall and I felt some misgivings about this family situation, where an aged mother in her 70s repeated in earnest how she wanted to return to her home village in the same way my own grandmother had once done. The next day we boarded the train to Kyoto and changed to another local train to Otsu, located by

rom left, my aunt, uncle, and cousin who never left Japan after the end of WWII (circa 1960s)

he largest lake, *Biwa*, in Japan, going through the extended unnels familiar to me from my childhood.

It was a dramatic reunion after all the happenings: he Korean War, and other devastations we had faced since eparating in 1945 after WWII. My aunt and uncle, Mrs. nd Mr. Lee, in their old age, managed their livelihood by ollecting scraps—cardboard boxes and other unused items ke utensils—in a *riaka*, or hand-driven pull cart. I was old my uncle Lee Kyong Dae (*Wonheng*), without a steady ob, had been a kind of gang leader, and had done things to venge the low wage Korean women workers in the Japanese otton industry.

The Lee family at the time, without a steady income, ere barely making ends meet and during my visit, Mr. Suzuki, heir son-in-law through my uncle's daughter, born of his *ekake* (concubine) was doing well with his automobile tire business. My "cousin," with the wherewithal to host me and the family in restaurants, took care of the expenses.

Both my aunt and uncle converted to Christianity after having practiced Korean shamanism for many years. Still, interestingly, my aunt's prayers in the church and a home, in essence used the same wording and pattern as before except in the name of Jesus Christ, our Lord.

My uncle chided my relative Cho for having been beguiled by the Communists, and told him to be good to hi mother so that she might fulfill her lifetime wish of returning to her hometown in Korea. Sadly, we found out that the family, in the midst of "the Patriotic Return to the Fatherland" inspired by the Korean Communists in Japan, went to North Korea and upon their arrival, Cho's mother said: "Is thi *Gunbuk*, my home village?" It was unfamiliar to her.

This return journey to Japan was one of the most unforgettable and rewarding trips of my life, reminiscing about the painful family experiences of the two wars, in combination with nostalgic fond encounters and past recollections of family and relatives. At Kyoto Station, my aunt and he family, grandson Lee Torao, and granddaughter Yoshimi, saw me off on the overnight express train *Kodama* to Tokyo. I hav never shed so many tears as I did on the train, encountering the emotional sensation of re-experiencing scenes of what went through in the fifteen years of separation from my aunt.

During the few days of my sojourn in Tokyo, I ha made arrangements to pay visits to some prominent persons related to statistics. I was able to pay respect to Professo Minobe Yokichi (later the Mayor of Tokyo) whom I had me at the 2nd Conference of Statisticians at ECAFE in 1958 i Bangkok. He was very pleased to see me and welcomed me t his office at Tokyo Education University (currently Tsukuba University), where he had moved after retirement from hi position in the Prime Minister's office. In his office, he staffe a tall handsome young man, Mr. Kawaii Saburo, Chief c

Division of Statistical Standards, who was later promoted to Director General and Vice Minister in the Prime Minister's Office. They arranged for me to visit the Japan Bureau of Statistics.

Director General Odawara, a prominent statistician, was kind enough to explain the functions of the Statistics Bureau and presented me with a signed copy of his famous book on statistics, authored when he was a professor at a major university. I believe Dr. Rice must have written to him prior to my departure from Washington D.C. Mr. Minobe had a close working relationship with Dr. Rice during his post-war statistical mission, and one weekend when I was invited to stay with the Rices, Mrs. Rice told me about an incident that took place during Mr. Minobe's visit to their Falls Church, Virginia home.

Staying in the guest room upstairs, which I was using, Mr. Minobe had used the bathroom as he would in Japan, washing outside the tub and splashing the water over his body. All the water leaked down to the kitchen. This was a fascinating cultural difference in bathing and we laughed over the result. As for my seeing Tokyo, Mr. Minobe asked Mr. Kawaii to be my guide and show me around Tokyo and the Ginza nightlife. Kawaii-san, who was the third son of a Zaibatsu family, and global heavy equipment manufacturer Komatsu Seisaku, picked me up at the hotel in a 1936 Mercedes Benz, his father's gift to him. I had a gorgeous time with him in Tokyo, and throughout his brilliant career, he and I were close professional and personal friends. Sadly he passed away a few years ago.

14

NO SUMMER VACATION TO IDLE AROUND

In August of 1960, I returned to Korea after completing th U.S. Department of Commerce training program and th requirements for my master's degree. This was only a fe months after the Changmyeon government came into powe As secretary of the National Census Council, I continued t assist the Rice Delegation, just as I was doing before leavin Korea for Washington, D.C. Subsequently I became a ful time member of the Advisory Group headed by Dr. Benjami Tepping, a prominent sampling statistician who was nom nated for Directorship of the University of Michigan Surve Research Center, representing Dr. Rice.

Ben Tepping and his wife, Ruth, were also first-ra musicians and contributed to the improvement of Seo Municipal Symphony Orchestra where Tepping was fir violist and his wife the first French horn. Additionally, the sponsored Kim Youngwook, a well-known violinist, to ent the Juilliard School of Music.

As part of my work, I compiled the first dictiona of statistical terminology in Korea along with several exper in the field, including Professor Byun Hyeong-yun of Seo National University Economics, and in collaboration wit rofessor Park Hong-Nae (PhD Statistics from University of Iorth Carolina) of Seoul National University Agriculture, anslated a textbook for modern inference statistics into orean, which was first used at Seoul National University to itroduce modern statistics.

After the May 16 Military Revolution in Korea in 961, I took part in the preparatory work for the first five-year conomic plan and prepared an English-language speech to be elivered at the White House by President Park Chung Hee uring his official visit to the United States as then Chairman f the Supreme Revolutionary Council.

When I left Korea for the University of Chicago in ebruary 1962, my successor was Dr. Han Seung Soo, who ccording to Dr. Tepping, did not quite fill my shoes. Years ter, he became deputy Prime Minister for Economy, and rime Minister.

While I was working for the Changmyeon govern-ient, I couldn't give up the idea of further academic pursuit. Iy determination to continue my advanced graduate work in ie United States grew all the stronger. Once I had started to ork with the Rice Statistical Mission in 1958, I exchanged tters on a regular basis with Dr. Rice when he was not in orea. He knew my intention to go abroad for study and was pparently impressed with my linguistic ability. I was pleased find out that he was searching for some possibilities for me get into one of the major schools in the US.

Six months before my first trip to Washington, D.C., e sent me a copy of a letter dated February 20, 1959, from ofessor Melville Herskovits of Northwestern University. It id: "Your young Korean sounds fine. Certainly, he sounds ke he has a natural ability for linguistics that he should be icouraged to develop, though I suspect with a mind like [his] e'll do outstanding work wherever he goes. I should say that

Dr. Rice, second from right (Korea, 1958)

Greenberg at Columbia, Hockett at Cornell, and Loundabur at Yale are the best people that we have, and they are all i good departments of anthropology, so if he is interested i some of the broader social science and cultural implication of language, he could get this work at either place."

Dr. Rice wrote to me in the margin of the letter: "Dea Joseph, I have written to all three of the men mentioned b Prof. Herskovits about you, also to another suggested b Margret Mead. Hope this meets your approval . . ."

After returning to Korea from the United States, I wa communicating with Dr. Rice by exchanging letters almos once a week and I asked him for his advice and suggestion about going back to the US for an advanced degree. As if h read my mind, Dr. Rice responded that he had already bee looking for a suitable school for me. He recommended th University of Chicago and Princeton University. I decided t go to the University of Chicago, which was ranked at the to in the social sciences.

Dr. Philip Hauser of University of Chicago (circa 1990s)

I entered the University of Chicago for the spring :mester in 1962. Professor Philip Hauser, Chairman of the epartment of Sociology, told me that he had received a long, ght-page letter of recommendation about me from his former rofessor, Dr. Stuart Rice, and urged me to study hard, adding at Chicago was not a party school like George Washington niversity.

Around that time, there were eight Korean students t the University of Chicago. Among them was Park Hee-bok, ho majored in mathematical statistics. Having graduated om Seoul National University as a top student, Park scared e, saying: "The graduate work at the University of Chicago is so impossibly difficult that no Korean ever received a doc torate degree in the field of social sciences." He suggested could leave with a master's to enroll at another school. Havin received this intimidating orientation from two individuals met for the first time in Chicago, my determination to succee in my graduate work in Chicago became dead serious.

The first semester was very difficult, as it had bee at George Washington University. Having worked every da without sleep until two or three in the morning, I was for tunate enough to receive satisfactory grades for the course I took. When the quarter ended and summer vacation wa about to start, I went to see my academic advisor, Professo Donald Bogue and told him I was worn out and would like t take a break to go to Washington, D.C., for a week. Professo Bogue sternly responded, "Do you think Chicago is a part school?" immediately pointing to the books on his offic bookshelves. He further admonished that summer vacatio in Chicago was not playtime, but rather an opportunity t do research during the day and read at night in preparatio for the preliminary examination. Assuming I had no work t do, he found work I could start on right on the spot. At tha moment, a memory long past struck me like lightning . . .

One time as a young middle school boy, I returned t my hometown. As soon as I came home, with the intention c taking a walk around the village, I put on my sneakers (spor shoes, more expensive) instead of changing into rubber shoe for work. Suddenly, out of nowhere, I heard my father's lou scolding voice. I had returned home after a long absence an now instead of giving a helping hand to the family, all I wa thinking about was playing? When I was denied a trip durin vacation time by Professor Bogue, this incident with my fathe dawned on me and I realized I could achieve my goal onl through tireless work and effort.

Studying at the University of Chicago was, in shor a continuation of my past life, chased by time. In addition t an incredible amount of required readings and selected reference materials, I had to write papers and reports. I always finished my quick simple meals and studied at the library in the evenings until the closing time of 11:00 p.m. Even after returning to the dormitory, I had to continue studying until about 2:00 a.m. As a result of my best effort, I was able to achieve satisfactory grades for the courses I took. About a year later, I was admitted to Chicago and awarded a generous scholarship that paid for my tuition, cost of living, and some book allowance. This made a remarkable difference compared to the research assistantship I had been living on. Gradually, I began to enjoy the campus and was no longer intimidated by its surroundings. I gained the "can do" confidence that I could make it through.

15

THE DREAM OF A HUNGRY BOY REALIZED

Achieving my doctoral degree course at the University of Chicago was like hell. At the final dissertation exam, in addition to the committee members, other Department professors came out to verify my qualifications for an academic appointment. My dissertation was an analysis of differential current fertility in the United States, later highlighted by the United Nations.

The University of Chicago is a private university founded by John D. Rockefeller. As a first in the field of natural science, it succeeded in the first nuclear fission experiment to open the twentieth-century atomic age. In the field of social science, it was the first to establish a department of sociology. Its departments of economics and anthropology are recognized as the best in the United States.

Chicago is also famous for being the university that requires the most rigorous written examinations. Particularly, the most difficult barrier in the PhD program is the preliminary exam, which lasts for four days. If one fails it, one has only one chance to retake it. In the first year of my admission, I learned from the Department that of ten students who took the exam, only two had passed.

The next barrier is the special field examination, which is also a written test. Only after passing two sets of exams, can a student prepare a dissertation proposal and make a presentation before the dissertation committee. The professors at the University of Chicago, an institution which emphasizes creativity, are very thorough in examining a dissertation proposal. They make it very difficult to pass. For some students this can take years. When the dissertation is completed, as the final step, the student defends it verbally.

From my second year at Chicago, I moved out of the International House and shared an apartment across the Midway with another Korean student, Yong-Ho Choe, now Emeritus Professor of History at the University of Hawai'i at Mānoa.[1] For food, at that time, we bought ox-tail, beef tongue, heart, and chicken, then inexpensive in the United States, and boiled them for *gomtang* soup. Although the scholarship was generous, I was frugal with my living expenses and saved. Then, a desperate letter came from my father, saying that after a major flood on the farm, the family might face the risk of starving. The money I saved was immediately sent home.

With the beginning of winter, things changed dramatically for the better. My graduate work was progressing well. I passed the important exams without difficulty and was assigned a desk to study at the research center even though I was still a student. At that time, I was given probably the best treatment as a graduate student. As I had some money to spare, I bought a used car for $250, which made my student life much more convenient.

The winter in Chicago is famous for its snow and severe cold. In winter, one has to place snow chains around one's car tires to prevent skidding on the frozen road.

1. Dr. Yong-Ho Choe passed away in May 2024.

I couldn't afford them, so I intentionally carried heavy bricks in the trunk to prevent the car from slipping. Due to many necessary repairs, my hands and clothes were frequently tainted with grease.

During that time, Professor Chung Beom Mo, the most capable leader in Korean education (his nickname was Corp., commander in education) had finished his master's degree in the early 1950s and was back at the University of Chicago as a PhD student. When I was hectically busy just before the final exams, Professor Chung suddenly appeared, asking me: "Do you have the courage to go watch a movie?" Then he added, "If you watch a couple of movies the day before the finals, your brain will rather clear up."

After that day, I would go to the movies with him before important exams and the results came out well. Chung also suggested that the two of us should demonstrate our ability to write our dissertations on topics related to research issues in the US on par with competing American students, unlike most Korean students in social sciences and humanities, who opted for Korean topics. We both did.

My religious background of Buddhism and traditional Confucian beliefs shifted toward Christianity upon my entrance to secondary school in Busan, thanks to my first home room teacher, Cho KwangJe, who happened to be a devout Christian. Occasionally I was invited to Cho's house on campus for lunch and before taking the food I had to follow the strange and unfamiliar verse of the hymn, *Bread of Life*. A few years later, I was encouraged to join the "Reconstruction Church," the most radical sect of the Korean Presbyterian Church, centered around the Christian martyrs who fought in jail against the Japanese religious oppression. The church was radical in that on Sundays the members had to abstain from public transportation, such as streetcars or buses, and walk to the church. This practice was based on a literal interpretation of the Biblical verse instructing no work on the Sabbath. The Korean Presbyterian Church treated other churches as houses of devils, since all of them obeyed Japanese colonial instructions and conformed to the practices of bowing before the Shinto shrines.

As a young boy, I valued the church's purity and devotion to faith and tried to live up to it, by fasting on Sundays as frequently as possible, and a couple of times fasting for three days without water. I was able to read through the whole Bible, the Old and New Testaments, and in 1959, during my training period, even made a trip from Washington, D.C., to an Amish community in Pennsylvania (with buggies driven by horses and gas lanterns for light) to observe an ideal model of a Christian church.

High school photo (circa 1952)

Subsequently, I observed ugly fights between the two dividing groups in my church, even using human feces, and I was truly disillusioned. Since then, I have been tormented with the question of where my spiritual home is, like in the famous Tang Dynasty poem "Yellow Crane Tower": "The sun is setting and where is my (spiritual) home?"

Professor Chung suggested we go together to listen to Paul Tillich's lecture series (he had moved from Harvard), and I complied. I was totally immersed in what Tillich said, word by word, on religious community instead of church; and that all religions—Judaism, Christianity, Buddhism, Islam, Hinduism, Shintoism (as he had spent some time in Japan)—are manifestations of the Ultimate Being. It was hard to control my tears in some moments when I sensed an exodus and liberation from the spiritual torment I was suffering. What was spoken so eloquently in a sonorous voice with a German accent could be rendered as a beautiful verbatim volume in print. After that, I read Tillich's works: *Courage to Be* and *Systematic Theology*, and took to heart his belief in "the God above the God of theism . . . *The courage to be is rooted in the God who appears when God has disappeared in the anxiety of doubt.*"

During my three and a half years at Chicago, I completed my master's and doctorate degrees. My master's thesis was published in the University of Chicago academic journal, and my doctoral dissertation on socioeconomic analysis of differential current fertility was published in the United States, and subsequently revised and expanded, published by the University of Chicago. The technical methodological part, later refined and extended, was highlighted by the United Nations Population Program for applications in both developing and developed countries.

As assistant professor at the University of Chicago (1964)

For my final dissertation defense, I was informed that in addition to my dissertation committee members, other Department professors would participate to ask broader sociological questions beyond my dissertation topic to verify my qualifications for an academic appointment in the Department.

Ultimately, I passed the final dissertation defense and was nominated for an assistant professor position. It was the moment when the dream of a hungry boy from a poor village was realized.

16

THE VIRTUE OF FORGETTING WHAT I GAVE AND REMEMBERING WHAT I RECEIVED

I was given an appointment to teach and research at the University of Chicago starting in the fall quarter of 1965. Teaching was challenging for me. I found the students in the class to be bright and sharp. Some of them went on to become prominent leaders in government and academic institutions. For example, one student in the US, Terry Sullivan, was President of the University of Virginia, until recently.

The following year in 1966, the Rockefeller Foundation, having provided a generous scholarship for my graduate study and funding the differential current fertility project, complained to the University about "brain drain" and in my case, recommended that as an obligation to the Foundation, I had to teach and research at Seoul National University for one year. As Lao-tzu said, "Loss can turn into a blessing."

Subsequently, this arrangement turned out to be a blessing for me in terms of my research as I was able to conduct some innovative methodological work in collaboration with Korea's government statistical office. While I was at SNU, I was also offered the position of Director of the Bureau of Statistics, where I could begin a professional career on the Economic Planning Board, headed by the Deputy Prime Minister. I declined by saying I wanted to continue my academic career.

After returning to Korea in early 1966, I went directly to my hometown and had a reunion with my family and village. I was surprised to find people from all over had gathered in the village, including the chief of Myon (the administrative district), the school principal, and family relatives and friends, all gathered for a feast to celebrate my "silver gown" return. My father said to the assembled guests, "My son's doctorate is just a bundle of straw soaked in water to weave a pair of sandals, and he has a big challenge before him to make a good pair of footwear in the future."

As my father envisioned, numerous important works followed and I continued to build on my research work. In 1967, the University of Michigan, in cooperation with Ford Foundation, sent me to Kuala Lumpur to serve as a senior advisor in population and development attached to the Prime Minister's Department in Malaysia. The Ford Foundation provided a large luxurious residence located in a high-class residential area (Jalan Madge, Ampang), an official car with a driver, as well as a private passenger car for personal use and a night guardsman (jagga). Thanks to the generous salary along with some representation budget, I was able to help my family in Korea.

In the 1960s, international travel was highly restricted for Koreans, mostly due to the scarcity of foreign currency, which had been mobilized to support the earlier phase of Korea's economic development. However, I was able to invite my parents to Kuala Lumpur.[1] It was their first trip ever to Southeast Asia. They traveled through Osaka, where our relatives welcomed them at the airport for a couple of days. An overnight layover in Hong Kong proved challenging because of the language barrier. They had instructions for navigating the immigration protocol and their hotel arrangements were hung around their necks with a lanyard.

On a shining balmy day (chilly, like early spring in Korea), I was relieved to welcome them in good health at the Kuala Lumpur Airport and have them settle down and change into light summer clothes at my residence. Coming from a cold country, they were so happy with the warm weather. I overheard my *amah* (maid) commenting that she washed the seventeen pieces of clothing my mother wore during her travels and hung them in the backyard for drying.

I asked my parents what they would enjoy doing during their stay. My father instantly said that he had been eating "vegetables all his life and would like to eat meat everyday." We bought all sorts of meat: steaks, cow hearts, tongue, stomach, tripe, tails, etc., along with one or two items from every menu, and he said he didn't need rice, but only *kimchi*.

1. Shortly after my parents' visit to Malaysia, the Korean Government, for the purpose of generating foreign currency, arranged with the Malaysian Ministry of Health for about fifty medical doctors to work in government hospitals in Malaysian cities. They were paid the equivalent of US $1500 per month, far more than they would earn in Korea, and some of them became good friends of mine, including Dr. Jeong, a retired Deputy Surgeon General of the Korean Army, who lived nearby with his family.

With my parents who visited Malaysia while I served as advisor to Prime Minister of Malaysia (1969)

Some days at the residence, I hosted guests for dinners and had my parents join the function. The traditional practice in Japan and Korea has been such that enjoying the food requires making a noise like slurping when eating noodles or making a "*susuri*" sound when drinking tea in Japan. I asked my father to cooperate in abstaining from making the "*chap chap*" sound, in front of the international guests when eating and he willingly said he would try. But after a few days he told me he just couldn't enjoy the delicious taste of meat without making this noise. I then told my father to enjoy the food the way he always wanted to. I can't forget the joy of staying together with my parents for a month.

At the time, there was a close affinity between the University of Chicago and the University of Michigan. In Chicago, the Michigan Department of Sociology was frequently referred to as "University of Chicago at Ann Arbor." During my stint in Malaysia as senior demographic advisor with the University of Michigan, Professor Ronald Freedman, on behalf of the Ford Foundation, and Professor Donald Bogue, came to visit me in Kuala Lumpur. We enjoyed a wonderful get-together. After my Malaysian assignment, which was challenging and fascinating, I returned to Chicago and worked closely with Bogue, as Associate Director of the Community and Family Study Center. The Center was founded by Earnest Burgess, one of the prominent leaders of the Chicago School of Sociology. Morris Janowitz was Chairman of Sociology.

While in Malaysia, it was an honor and pleasure for me to host Professor Lee Jong Woo, President of Korea University, and Mrs. Lee (Choo Gukhee, Professor of Education at Ewha University) at my residence for a week. Lee Jong Woo had kindly and generously offered me a full professorship during my affiliation with Seoul National University in 1966. Another happy occasion was my hosting of Professor Yang Jae Mo, Vice President of Yonsei University for Medicine and a pioneer in the Korean family medicine program. I enjoyed kicking a soccer ball with him in the backyard of the residence. Dr. Yang had made a special trip to the University of Chicago campus on his way back to Korea at the suggestion of the Population Council to see me during my third year of graduate study in Chicago.

Dr. Yang and Professor Park Dae Sun, President of Yonsei University, who also came to Kuala Lumpur, offered me a full professorship with a plan for me to lead in the establishment of a new sociology department at Yonsei. I managed to decline the offer, but when Yonsei afterward established its department of Sociology, I assisted the University by recommending my able former students who then developed it into a leading department in Korea. Subsequently, Professor Park, who was also a leading theologian, became my good friend. My wife, Eun-Ja Cho, and I were honored to have him preside over our wedding ceremony in 1973 in Seoul, Korea, since President Park was well acquainted with my future father-in-law, Chun Taik Bu who served as the Secretary General of YMCA of Korea.

Wedding photo with my wife, Eun-Ja Cho, with Dr. Park Daesun officiating (1972)

From left, my father-in-law (Chun Taik Bu), my father (Cho Sam Soo), my mother (Park Kyung Doo), and my mother-in-law (Han Choon Hak, circa late 1980s)

Malaysia, including the Singapore territory, became an independent nation after World War II and Singapore subsequently seceded to become a sovereign state. Malaysia was and still is a multiethnic nation. When I worked there in 1967, its ethnic composition was composed of slightly less than one half indigenous Malays, about 35 percent Chinese, about 15 percent Indians and others. Endowed with plentiful natural resources in agriculture and minerals, the country, with its tropical climate, actually benefited from British colonial rule, which contributed to the development of its infrastructure in transportation, public health, education, and civil service systems. Economically, South Korea in the late 1960s was far behind Malaysia, with a per capita GNP of US $140 in 1966 and US $190 in 1968—less than one half compared with US $400 for Malaysia, although Korea surpassed Malaysia not too many years later.

At the request of the Government, I made some population projections for the country of Malaysia, with the assumption of the then-prevailing fertility and mortality rates; namely, a higher fertility for the Malays than the Chinese and Indians. The results showed the Malay population would exceed 50 percent in less than a decade and the Government was so pleased that my population statistics appeared in the top news in all of the major national media.

Malaysia's Prime Minister then was Tunku Rhaman, educated at Oxford and a gentle and open-minded leader. In his cabinet, the Finance Minister was always Chinese as China dominated the economic and business life of the country. I still remember an anecdote attributed to Rahman's speech encouraging his Malay ethnic group to work harder. It goes like this: "When there is one Chinese, he will start building a factory and if another Chinese comes along, then another factory will be built, and so on. When there is one Indian, he will build a factory, and two Indians will build two factories and three Indians will form a labor union. When there is one Malay, he will take a nap and two Malays will take a double nap as one wakes up to see the other still sleeping. Three Malays will further extend sleeping hours."

The Prime Minister was cognizant of some basic ethnic characteristics and tendencies (Chinese diligence, Indian facility in verbal communication, and the Malay's relaxed outlook and attitude) and in the Asian manner, he tried to inculcate the value of work by means of self-criticism as a Malay. Also notable is the fact that the Minister of Labor was consistently Indian in Rahman's administration.

There are very few harmonious multiethnic and multiracial societies in the world. Hawai'i is one example. Countries and cities with multi-ethnic populations have experienced numerous incidents of explosive riots and tragedies over their history. Malaysia is no exception. In 1969, when I was still in Malaysia, a tragic racial riot broke out and unwittingly I was right in the middle of it, in harm's way.

The result of the riots was thousands of deaths and serious injuries, mostly between Malays and Chinese, with the former burning the Chinese stores and houses on the outskirts of Kuala Lumpur, along with their occupants, and the latter killing and maiming Malays in the city.

One evening, I was having dinner with my newly-arrived assistant from the University of Michigan, Lois Vebrugge, who later taught at Johns Hopkins University and is now emeritus distinguished Professor, at the University of Michigan. The Chinese woman who prepared our dinner made an emergency request for a ride to the *Ipoh* market area of her residence in the central city, where she found out some trouble had occurred. I instantly obliged, and Lois wanted to join us for a ride. The Chinese cook, in her red Chinese coat, sat on the right seat and Lois sat in the back seat of the Ford Foundation car arranged for my private use. From Jalan Madge, the street of my residence, I drove for a few minutes to enter Ampang Ring Road. After only a few minutes' drive toward the central city, I saw a group of young Malays with barongs (large scythes with long handles) and other gadgets like pipes waving at us to stop our vehicle. I instinctively felt a deadly aggression in the confrontation and I pressed my gas pedal and sped through them. They hacked my car, breaking the side and the rear. If I had stopped, with the Chinese woman beside me in the car, we would have suffered the same fate as many Chinese, killed inside a burning car.

This was near the Kampong Baru ("new village") built for the Malays. Instead of going further, I took a right turn on Gurney Road, heading toward a military camp where I remembered that a colleague of mine, Douglas Keare of the Harvard Advisory Group, lived. We went to his house, and his wife Ginger, trembling with her children, welcomed us and told me that Douglas was away on a trip to East Malaysia (Northern Borneo). We stayed there for the night without much sleep, fearfully watching young Malay men in groups going around searching for Chinese houses to burn and Chinese to kill. Ginger had a number of her Chinese friends taking refuge in the house. The next morning, realizing that no harm was done during the night and all of us were safe in the house, we shared a sigh of relief. I communicated with the official responsible for looking after me as Government Advisor, and he told me that his office would arrange for our secure return to my residence.

A little before noon, a military contingent of two vehicles, one of them a heavily armored vehicle with a machine gun, came to Keare's house. They escorted my car, with one armored vehicle in front and one in the rear, back to my residence. This was the first and last time I have ever driven behind an armored car providing for my security.

Malaysia and Kuala Lumpur came under an emergency decree and people were required to stay home as though in a pandemic, although their safety was not guaranteed at home. The Korean Embassy provided a Korean flag for me to attach to my car so that I would not be perceived as Chinese. The Ford Foundation office suggested I go to Singapore for a while to get away from the chaotic situation in Kuala Lumpur, and the Korean Embassy arranged for my transportation to the airport. In Singapore, I stayed at the Hotel Singapura and was able to do some work poolside. It was relaxing after all the stress and turmoil in Malaysia.

After this historic riot, resulting in enormous casualties, with deaths reaching almost ten thousand, the post-Tunku regimes took more rigorous measures to support the native Malays, implementing the "Bumiputra policy," a quota system in which government employment was more favorably extended to the Malays, and employed in government-related economic and industry sectors. Consequently, there was an exodus of talented Chinese and Indian individuals, which in the long run had negative implications economically and politically. This policy went against what Deng Xiaoping, the

Chinese leader who opened the Chinese economy, preached: "According to one's ability and one's need." The policy also ignored the hard lessons learned from the American experience of the quota system for the Black minority. As I occasionally repeat: "Culture precedes ideology."

A recollection regarding Singapore: One day in Malaysia, a local young Chinese woman who was working as a maid at my official residence was reading the *Namyang Sambao* (南洋商報), the major Singapore newspaper in Chinese characters. I asked if she really understood Chinese and she replied "yes." At that moment, I felt that she was more knowledgeable than me—a boy who had grown up within the Chinese cultural sphere and earned a doctorate. I decided then to study Chinese. In 1981, when I led the delegation as President of the East-West Center in Hawai'i on an official visit to China, I felt rewarded for my effort. For me, the trip to China was a meaningful, historic trip—the first visit ever of a Korean national to China since the end of WWII, and understood to be the first step toward the Korea-China relations.

Now in retrospect, I return to the teaching of the grand Chinese historian Sima Qian in "The Recording of History, Xinlingjun" (*Volume 77*): *"Forget what you have given to others but remember only the virtue of having received from others,"* and I realize that I should not forget what so many people have given to me.

During my horticultural middle school days, I learned the Christian spirit from my teacher Mr. Cho Kwang-je, and from our teacher of agriculture and forestry, Mr. Hyun Gyutaek, I learned the Confucian lesson of "five man": "A man is not a man and if a man does not behave like a man, he is not a man."

I can't forget Colonel Merrit Briggs and Colonel Ivan Cooper, commanders of the 2nd US Chemical Mortar Battalion, with whom I spent my critical teenage boyhood years in the battle zone facing life and death at the forefront of the Korean War. I am also indebted to Professor Robert Rainer of the University of Foreign Studies for having taught me proper English language and literature. I am truly saddened by my inability to pay back what Dr. Stuart Rice gave me as my mentor in guiding and supporting my education in the United States.

Above all, I can't forget my father who passed on to me the virtue of honesty. As the first part of my story comes to a close, I would like to end with a memorial poem that characterizes my father, who passed away in 1986. This poem, written by prominent poet Mr. Ku Sang, was based on the stories shared by my father's hometown neighbors and family members, which were put together by my wife.

> He spent all his life hidden in the remote
> countryside.
> With an upright heart and outstanding wisdom
> He was always a guiding light to the villagers.
> Endowed with diligence and frugality by nature
> He gave graceful care to kinsmen and neighbors
> young and old
> Beyond the horizon, we see his passing, leaving us
> yearning all the more.

> 초야에 한 평생을 묻혀 사셨으되,
> 하 곧은 마음씨와 뛰어난 그 슬기로
> 언제나 마을 사람의 길잡이가 되셨네
> 부지런과 알뜰을 천성으로 지니시고
> 위 아래 일가 이웃 극진히 보살피시니
> 북망에 드시고 나매 그 그리움 더하네

At the memorial stone for my father with my wife, Eun-Ja Cho (2016)

The benevolent lessons I learned in Malaysia served as an unforgettable lifetime guide. I cannot express in words my gratitude to my American friends whom I met in the military and in the United States, and my father who taught me the virtue of honesty. I now wanted to live by the virtue of remembering what I received from others.

Part II

17

SEOUL NATIONAL UNIVERSITY AND THE UNIVERSITY OF MICHIGAN

Two years after the Tokyo Summer Olympics of 1964, I had the chance to experience the post-Olympic mood in Japan, which was invigorating economically as well as politically, and Japan was rising again in the world, as I anticipated it would during my college days, while refreshing my Japanese. Japan was enjoying mutually beneficial economic cooperation with its Asian neighbors Korea, Taiwan, Hong Kong, and Singapore—"newly industrializing countries (NIA)," the so-called "little tigers."

During the Tokyo Olympics, I was truly touched to find out that the NHK Symphony Orchestra was commemorating the closing event of the Olympics with a live, nationwide performance from Korean Fantasy. This piece had been the Korean national anthem since its independence, and it was composed by Maestro Ahn Eak-tai in a chorus using the original Korean words. The fascinating background story surrounding this event was later broadcast in a KBS (Korean Broadcasting System) television series and the story was personally confirmed for me by Mr. Maeda Yoshinari, founding Chairman of NHK, who later served as a member of the Board of Governors of the East-West Center. Along with his wife, Mr. Maeda became an intimate friend of mine and when he passed away, I represented the East-West Center at his funeral in Tokyo.

According to Mr. Maeda, at the time of the Tokyo Olympics, Ahn was the most famous of Asian ethnic conductors, with a strong patriotic spirit for the national liberation of Korea from Japanese colonial rule. He trained under German composer Richard Strauss. The story is as follows: Ahn, with great ambition, went to Europe to study music, determined to study under Strauss and tried hard to get an appointment to see him. It was not unusual that such an appointment was not easily granted, and Ahn decided to wait in front of the Strauss residence every day to try his luck. On a hot summer day, the children of the Strauss family were swimming in the lake in front of their house, and one of them was drowning. Ahn instantly jumped into the lake and saved the child. The composer came out and greatly appreciated Ahn's courageous act in saving his grandchild. He gladly accepted Ahn as his student, and the protégé later became a prominent conductor sought after by major orchestras in Europe.

For all the performances Ahn engaged in in the major European cities, he always made it a condition for his role to end his performance with the refrain from his Korean Fantasy. On one occasion in Rome, Italy, in which he was to conduct the Orchestra of Rome before the end of WWII, the Japanese military secret service found out about the event and prepared to kidnap and arrest Ahn. Italy at that time was a member of the Axis powers along with Germany. Mr. Maeda, at the time, was Chief of the European Bureau for Asahi Shimbun. As a fan and friend of Ahn, he conceived a plan to help him escape the Japanese Kenpei's attempted capture, immediately after he finished his Korean Fantasy. The plan succeeded.

In advance of the Tokyo Olympic performance, Ahn's patriotic insistence on including Korean Fantasy was a real challenge for Mr. Maeda, who on one hand, recognized Ahn as the most prominent Asian conductor of his time, and on the other, had to convince NHK Board members who opposed the condition of Korean Fantasy as the finale of the symphonic performance. Mr. Maeda, using the examples of Sibelius's *Finlandia* and Smetana's *My Homeland* as artistic expressions of the national spirit, was able to persuade the Symphony's board to agree with the plan for the Tokyo Olympics commemorating performance with Ahn Eak-tai as conductor. I wish something like this was happening today between Japan and Korea as the relationship between the two countries in recent years has deteriorated to a contemptible level.

Upon returning to Seoul, I settled myself at Mr. Roh Yong Kyu's house for different intervals, as a lodger in a small room over a number of years. Roh, my senior colleague and long-time friend (he passed away many years ago) had served in the Ministry of Reconstruction from 1958 and offered me his place. I have tried to compensate his family in kind since, but I still feel indebted to them.

One day in late February of 1966, I went to the College of Liberal Arts and Sciences at Seoul National University located at the SNU Medical School near Jongro 5-ga, the previous location of the Keijo (Seoul in Japanese) Imperial University during the colonial period. I made courtesy visits to the appropriate offices, starting with Professor Lee Hae Yong of Sociology and the Director of the newly established Population Study Center. He graciously worked out an arrangement with the Population Council in consultation with Professor Vincent Whitney of the University of Pennsylvania for my assignment at SNU and I was led to my new office in the main College building.

Professor Lee studied at the Population Study Center at the University of Pennsylvania for his masters and he was a member of the direct descendants of the Li Dynasty royal family. On some social occasions, he would complain to me about his relatives. Except for him and a few others, about one hundred of them had been without any gainful employment or earning income since the end of the Dynasty. Many of them would come to him for spending money for cigarettes, transportation, and other incidentals, implying that work was not on their menu, but being served and cared for was.

Before departing Chicago, I had packed all my books and research materials in small packages as specified by the U.S. Post Office and mailed some fifty parcels; most of them arrived to pile up in my office. A sophomore student from the Sociology Department, Kim Sun Ung, was suggested to assist me in unpacking and fixing up the office, and it took a few days to get the office in shape. In 1966, Korea was still a poor developing country and I was to get a salary roughly equivalent to USD $250 a month, the pay level of an associate professor from the University. I was also fortunate to continue to receive a monthly stipend of $400 from the University of Chicago for continued work in connection with the US differential fertility project, a stipend which paid for my roundtrip travel from Chicago.

All my books, including new books hard to acquire in Korea, were stacked in the walls of the bookshelves in my office and a week later I entered the office on a Monday to find all the bookshelves cleaned out and empty. I immediately notified the University security guard who told me he would notify the police and investigate the burglary. Later in the day, the security guard informed me that he found piles of books on the roof of a nearby building and both of us climbed up to the roof to find the books from my office. The security guard told me that the burglar must have known the value of the new books and probably thought he could get good prices for them. I was very disheartened when the books disappeared, but the recovery of them really gave me psychological relief. It was hard to guess who did it. An insider who knew about the new books, or a student with a collaborator?

A few days later the student Kim, who had heard about the burglary incident, came to my office, deploring the situation, and made an offer to sleep in my office at night if I would buy him a thick sleeping bag from the East Gate Market (*Dongdaemun Shijang*). This would be of some help to him. His father had died early and he was the only son, with his poor mother working as a maid for another family. He would otherwise have to pay for his lodging somewhere. Having been in a poverty-stricken situation myself, I took great pity on him and gave him the money to buy the sleeping bag, providing whatever I could to help him survive and continue his studies. Years later he succeeded in coming to the US to obtain his doctorate in Sociology, and I was able to help him enter the Korea Development Institute (KDI), a premier national research institution, as the first non-economist researcher. He later transferred to Hanyang University and retired as chairman of its Sociology Department.

I relate an interesting phenomenon of an undesirable academic culture that I experienced for the first time at SNU. It had to do with teaching and nepotism in faculty recruitment, especially within the College of Liberal Arts and Sciences (*Mullidae*). I was assigned to teach a course in statistics and according to Kim Sun Ung, there was a rumor going around among the students and some faculty in the Sociology Department that a new faculty member would be teaching (referring to me), not ever having "put a foot at the gate of SNU" as a student. Having not matriculated at SNU, it was implied that I was not fit to teach. I was thereby actively breaking the tradition and practice of exclusion as the first American PhD in social science to teach for the College and I may have contributed to the opening up of their "hermit academic department."

Dr. Yoo Ki Cheon, President of Seoul National University, a scholar with a doctorate in Law who married a well-known American legal scholar (both attended Yale), welcomed me enthusiastically to my role and told me on a train trip that an international academic like me should be a pillar of the University in future. He also mentioned that in the *Mullidae* (문리대—College of Liberal Arts)[1] there were a few departments that were abusing the tradition in such a way as to promote a selfish interest on the part of mediocre faculty and assistants. He named a couple of "forever lecturers" who would never dare to go abroad for higher degrees, preferring to instead stay "inside" providing personal service to the professors who helped them obtain degrees. He said: "Their appointments will never be approved so long as I remain President."

Dr. Yoo was a graduate of Tokyo University Law School, the most prestigious law school before and after WWII in Japan. He said some SNU colleges, particularly *Mullidae*, were abusing the Keijo (Seoul) Imperial University practice, claiming it as the direct institutional inheritor when other schools had been subsumed in the course of the establishment of the new Seoul National University. He added that the top national universities in Japan such as Tokyo and Kyoto would not adhere to the same practice to the detriment of academic quality.

From my lodging at Ahyeon-Dong, I walked every day about six kilometers to the *Mullidae* instead of getting on a crowded bus. There was no subway then and I avoided messy traffic in the central street of *Jongro*.

In Seoul, the academic year starts in March, and in 1966, as I was about to go to the classroom to teach my course, Kim warned me that nobody would be in the classroom according to the tradition and practice of the College. A few classes later, the students would appear in the classroom.

---

1. *Mullidae* was the name of the College of Liberal Arts at Seoul National University from 1946 to 1975. The modern equivalent is the College of Arts and Sciences.

One day in April, when the cherry blossoms were in full bloom, I went to teach and found only one student sitting in the class. He told me that he was representing the class, most of whom were celebrating the cherry blossoms at Changyong Palace. If I insisted on teaching, he would listen to the lecture on his classmates' behalf. I told the student to join the celebration.

Toward the end of the semester, I administered the final written examination during which I caught two students cheating. I tore up their exam papers and threw them in the trash. The two students were the graduates of Gyeonggi, the top high school in Seoul. After attending Gyeonggi, when one graduates to SNU, one acquires the euphemistic title "KS," akin to a green light for upward social mobility. I was getting ready to submit the final grades to the academic affairs office when I gave flunking grades to these two students. I had to face entreaties from their high school classmates as well as a friendly request from a faculty member of KS. Among the students I taught in the class, I found the students who came from provincial schools to enter SNU were, on the whole, of higher quality and had potential for intellectual growth, compared to many bright and able students from Gyeonggi who were "too smart" (*yakda* in Korean) as was the generally accepted impression in the upper social strata in Korea.

In the course of the first semester, I was assigned one formal assistant, Lee Mun Woong, and subsequently another, the only female junior student in her class, Roh Mihye (KS), and of course, the volunteer Kim Sun Ung, who slept in my office. I applied for a little grant through SNU to the Population Council in New York for "*a survey of vital events of births and deaths in a rural community*" in the *Bopsu Myon* rural district that included my home village. The survey also included questions related to community leadership in the acceptance of family planning, and the grant proposal was approved. An increasing number of students wanted to participate in the survey project and five were selected, all of whom spent time working in the village and stayed in the side room of my parents' house. All of them enjoyed the survey work, as well as the rural way of life, and since four or five had to sleep in the same room, there was one student who every night before bedtime asked his bedfellows to tie his wrists together tightly with a broomstick to prevent him hitting others with his aggressive sleeping habit.

In the course of my year's stint at SNU, I ended up having eleven assistants, both formal and volunteers, all of whom came to my crowded office and sought my counsel, guidance, and support for their future education. For example, Lee Mun Woong wanted to study in the US and I arranged for him to go on a scholarship to study at Rice University where one of my Chicago classmates was teaching. After his doctorate, Lee returned to SNU's Anthropology Department and retired as emeritus. My assistant, Miss Roh Mihye, was later accepted by the University of Minnesota, but wanted to go to the University of Chicago for its perceived "higher prestige." Understanding the ego-oriented student culture at *Mullidae*, I helped her go to Chicago when I returned there. After earning a masters in Sociology, she worked for the National Institute for Health and Social Welfare and finished her career as Director of Equal Opportunity (Gender) for the Seoul Special City Government.

In the fall semester of 1966, Professor Chung Beom Mo (who shared time together with me in Chicago as a graduate student watching movies before exams) worked out an arrangement for an intercollegiate graduate course on interdisciplinary social science with the university leadership, open not only to the College of Arts and Science, but also to the schools of education, commerce, and public health in the medical school. There were about twenty graduate students of high quality and caliber from the different schools and I really enjoyed teaching the course. Some of them later became prominent leaders of research and academic institutions, as well as Cabinet members, and in one instance, a Deputy Prime Minister. Professor Chung also had me lecture on several occasions in retraining programs for the leaders of the secondary schools nationwide.

As mentioned earlier, I was offered a faculty position from both Yonsei and Korea University during my time at Seoul National University and not long after, Professor Lee Hae Yong, as head of the academic affairs of SNU, made me an offer which I politely declined as I was becoming more involved in international research activities.

Relevant to my international research, the United Nations Economic and Social Commission for Asia and the Pacific (UNESCAP), prior to my return to Chicago, inquired whether I would be interested in a position in the Population Division, a comfortable assignment with job security and a stable income in a developing country setting in Bangkok. I did not send my CV as requested. In my whole academic career, I never engaged in salary negotiations for my positions with a belief that I would be provided with an adequate income to maintain a comfortable living, in contrast to the hardships in my past. Recently I was pleased to learn that Nitobe Inazo (more on this later) whose photograph was imprinted on the Japanese banknote of 5000 yen manifested a similar Confucian value in his writings, encouraging younger generations toward a bigger vision and goal.

In connection with my professional affiliation with the Korean Bureau of Statistics beginning in the late 1950s, I maintained a long lasting network of colleagues and friends over decades, some of whom continued a very close professional and personal relationship with me.

One of the most remarkable relationships was my lifetime bond with Dr. Chung Soo Bong, Chairman of the Board of Directors of the Dong-A University in Busan, who passed away about ten years ago after serving as President of the University for a number of years. He was my superior in the Division of Statistical Standards of the Statistics Bureau in the Ministry of Home Affairs, which was subsequently subsumed under the newly established Economic Planning Board (EPB) and headed by a Deputy Prime Minister. During this time in 1958, I was sent to the Statisticians Meeting in Bangkok. Chung Soo Bong, along with Bureau Director Lim Chun Shik's secretary, Miss Byun saw me off at the Yeouido Airport, the first small international airport in Korea, with a bouquet of flowers on behalf of our Director. Shortly after my joining the Bureau, Chung graciously offered for me to stay at his modest Korean style house in *Donam-dong* in a side room while he and his wife shared the main *ondol* room with two toddler boys. He wanted to have conversations with me while going to and from work together, to intermittently learn some English from me. We mostly travelled in a *Shibal* (starting) taxi, the first manufactured car in Korea utilizing used drum barrels for a body. I remember that hot summer fondly, where I was well fed and generously taken care of.

One of the toddlers, Sang Hee, used to call me "Say Yes Uncle" (politely, *NyeKe* in Busan dialect). Under my guidance, he finished his graduate education in Hawai'i and completed his academic career as a professor. He is currently Secretary of the Dong-A University Board.

When I came to SNU early in 1966, I made a visit to Dong-A University Campus and was very happy to see him working as Director of Academic Affairs following his government service in the Ministry of Affairs as Director of General Affairs. I also paid respect to Founding President Chung Jae Hwan of Dong-A University. The Chungs were very pleased about my doctorate from Chicago and the wherewithal of my subsequent success. Chung asked me if it was possible for me to lecture on a regular basis at Dong-A during my one-year visiting appointment with SNU. I was pleased with the offer, but at the same time felt it would be a challenge to commute from Seoul. Dong-A was at the time the largest and best-known University south of the Han River in Korea. I agreed to teach using the weekends, by starting on Friday and returning to Seoul on Sunday.

Consequently, I would get on an overnight express train (*Tongilho*) which took about twelve hours to get to Busan. Arriving on a Friday, I would check in at the University Guest House and start teaching an interdisciplinary class with between seventy and a hundred students and the next day, Saturday, did some variation of a teaching arrangement, after which I would return to Seoul on Sundays. I enjoyed the interaction with the students and this facility during my stint in Busan. I found the top twenty-five percent of the students at Dong-A were just as academically adept as those in my class at SNU. One student, Cho Moo Jae, later became a justice of the Korean Supreme Court.

For two days a week during fall semester lectures in Busan, the Chung family invited me to stay at the President's Residence, where his parents occupied the main upper structure and I shared the lower part with Chung since his wife was still in Seoul looking after their children's education. This was the beginning of my lifelong relationship with Dong-A University.

18

THE OWN CHILDREN METHODOLOGY

The Own Children Method (OCM),[1] simply put, can be described as generating dynamic moving pictures from a one-time snapshot—a still picture of a census or survey. The household roster on the entrance of a house can provide you with an image similar to a family photo in which you can imagine your younger mother when you were born—reverse survival in action. The censuses and surveys are one-time snapshots of the households and families for large and/or sizable populations.

The OCM's use of census information has been described in the UN Manual X, *Indirect Techniques for Demographic Estimation* as follows: " . . . probably the greatest innovation introduced by the proponents of the own-children method is the exploitation of seldom-used census information for fertility estimation purposes."[2]

---

1. For a simplified explanation of the OCM, see Dr. Robert Retherford's contribution in part 3, chapter 22.

2. Manual X, *Indirect Techniques for Demographic Estimation*, United Nations Department of International Economic and Social Affairs, 1983, p. 182. This quote is footnoted in Manual X with the following citation: Lee-Jay Cho, *The own-children approach to fertility estimation: an elaboration*, International Population Conference, Liege. 1973 (Liege, International Union for the Scientific Study of Population, vol. 2, pp. 263–280.)

Family photo (1989), shown as an example of reverse survival in action

The background is as follows. As a PhD student at the University of Chicago in the early 1960s, having spent a year at the U.S. Census Bureau as a trainee in 1959, and with some background in economic statistics and census in the Korean government, I wanted to work on a dissertation using census and survey data. My MA thesis, on the estimation of "refined measures of fertility," used variables such as child-women ratios and infant mortality for the countries of the world. Published in *Demography* in 1964, my thesis was aimed at using "refined measures" over the crude measurements available at the time. The substance and data of this article was later included in the book *The World Economy* by Walt Rostow, who taught at MIT and served as Security Advisor to Presidents Kennedy and Johnson. I was honored to

With Professor Don Bogue (2009)

receive Walt's call for my permission. Afterwards we became good professional friends, sharing some illuminating dialogue on Korean economic development in its take-off stage under President Park Chung Hee.

Professor Don Bogue, my thesis advisor; Philip Hauser; and Nathan Keyfitz (who later went to Berkeley, but was then at EWPI at the University of Hawai'i and finally retired at Harvard) suggested I spend one summer working with Wilson Grabill, Head of the Fertility Branch at the Census Bureau in the Population Division headed by Paul Glick, a friend of mine.

Having developed a network of professional friends and a working relationship under the aegis of Dr. Stuart A. Rice, Wilson Grabill was an unusually competent demographer specializing in fertility, and a wonderful person—an angel. Wilson was deaf and could hardly speak. He graduated from the Gallaudet College of Deaf and obtained an MA in Statistics from American University, in Washington, D.C., He was like *Britain's Got Talent's* "Lost Voice Guy" Lee Ridley. I managed to learn some sign language and we communicated with "*Pildam*, Brush talk" written notes. The U.S. Census Bureau was then one of the most innovative and pioneering think tanks—employing Hansen, Hurwitz, and Ben Tepping in sampling, for example.

Wilson was interested in the ratios of own-children under 5 and 5–9 years of age to women of childbearing ages of 15–54, and interpolating the ratios to obtain the 5-year average age-specific fertility rates (ASFR) for the period 5 years and 5–9 years prior to the census. Wilson and I worked on interpolating the child-to-women ratios to estimate the average ASFR for the two 5-year periods preceding the 1960 US census, and this methodological work was published in *Demography in 1965*. Further methodological refinements were completed as I finished my doctoral dissertation "Differential Current Fertility in the United States," subsequently published as a monograph by the University of Chicago in 1970.

At the time, differential fertility was a controversial issue, involving prominent scholars like Nobelist Gary Becker, with Kingsley, Judith Davis, and others arguing *"Is a baby a consumer good?"* and *"Does poverty beget poverty?"* The measurement of differential current fertility by income and other SES status was important for providing the empirical basis for explanation.

During my assignment at SNU, I was appointed as a member of the Korean Statistical Commission. My friend Hahm Manjhun, an economic statistician from the Bank of Korea, was Director of the Bureau of Statistics and he asked me to cooperate with the U.S. Census Bureau on technical issues of population census and surveys, age data, undercount, sampling, and more.

At the U.S. Census Bureau, the idea that any tabulation plan and changes thereto need several stages of approval was reinforced by my earlier service as a member of the U.S. census advisory committee. In Korea, with my friend as the director of statistics, I enjoyed the freedom to discover new tabulations for methodological experimentations, for example, "own children" tabulations, which informed the development of the Own Children Method (OCM); this was a blessing. During that same year, I did the fertility and family planning survey with my students at SNU in my hometown, in remote villages in rural Korea. Years later in the 1970s, I took the East-West Population Institute (EWPI) Summer Seminar participants to the same villages. The participants included Peter McDonald of Australia National University (ANU), who mentioned his visit in his presidential speech for IUSSP in Busan a few years ago.

There are both cultural and historical influences on the OCM. During my childhood during the war years in Japan, I witnessed the tense social environment in which the population was highly regimented and the households and their members had to be strictly accounted for. In the entrance of each house, a plate must show, for each of the family members, their full names, birth dates, and relationship to the head of the household. As I have stated, as a child, I used to have this information sewn onto the upper part of my jacket. This practice is based on a practice that has a long history in the countries of the Chinese cultural sphere and it's a good example of "Shumon-Aratamecho" as documented by Susan Handley of the University of Washington in her work on Japanese history.

In my own village, there remained some legacy of this practice after World War II when we did our village survey.

The Korean Statistics Bureau cooperated in re-tabulating the census data on own children in single years by the single years of mothers based on relationships in the family for fifteen and twenty years prior to the census. Because of some of the problems demographers will appreciate, I chose fifteen years prior to the time of the census.

I had arrived in Malaysia in the final phase of the 1967 Malaysian Fertility Survey, which was conducted by the Malaysian Government, the National Family Planning Board, and the Department of Statistics, in collaboration with the University of Michigan. The survey team was led by James Palmore (my classmate at Chicago) of the Michigan Sociology Department and the Population Studies Center, under the direction of Professor Ronald Freedman (also a Chicago alumnus), my boss in Malaysia for this phase of the analysis of the survey data. The survey team included two competent research assistants, doing their PhDs at Michigan, which, for a short period of time, overlapped with the initial phase of my work. Allen Schnaiberg later became Professor at Northwestern University and passed away as emeritus, and Chris Langford from England became Professor of Demography in the Department of Social Policy at London School of Economics.

I was warmly welcomed in Kuala Lumpur by relevant institutions, but I sensed some hesitation on the part of Dr. Ariffin bin Marzuki (MD), the Director of the National Family Planning Board (NFPB), supported by Chairman of the Board, Khir Johari, concurrently Minister of Education, who ranked only behind the Deputy Prime Minister. Both turned out to be wonderful people with whom I enjoyed a cordial friendship.

Ariffin was trained in the UK and married a beautiful Welsh nurse who was kind and sociable. In the course of undertaking the survey and at the final stage, apparently some sensitive issues had emerged between the survey team and NFPB and thereby soured the relationship somewhat with Michigan. During his short trip to Kuala Lumpur, Ron Freedman experienced a tough time in trying to talk to Dr. Ariffin, to gain the approval of the release of the survey data for analysis, and Ariffin was essentially stonewalling Ron; for instance by having him wait for half an hour in front of the Director's office. A great deal was at stake. The success of the survey project would be undermined if the data was not released for the analytic stage, and this, for Ron, was a formidable challenge.

At the time there was a medical doctor from University of Michigan's School of Public Health, Ralph Tenhave, Michigan Dutch on assignment on public health and family planning, who used to refer to Ron Freedman as the "god of fertility" for having developed one of the most successful population studies programs in the US, focused on Taiwanese studies of family planning and fertility transition. Ralph (a jolly good person) and I shared much fun and jokes together and he empathized with me on what Ron Freedman was facing and going through.

Gradually I found out the root of the problem, and simply put, it was related to cultural and attitudinal differences in handling the survey and the plan for the analysis. Jay Palmore was a son of the Christian missionary in the Philippines with a BA from Oberlin, who came to Chicago for his PhD and afterwards went to teach at Michigan. In Malaysia, I saw Jay together with his wife, Sandy, and their baby daughter. Jay was satisfied with the successful completion of the survey, which contained valuable sets of data on a variety of topics related to fertility, marriage, family, community, and numerous other sociodemographic variables. He was not aware of potential issues in connection with the survey data that might emerge in the near future, and he was more than complacent, having thoroughly fulfilled the scope of work for the survey utilizing the staff at the Department of Statistics. Dorothy Fernandez, head of the Population Statistics Branch, who also worked for me, had a fond impression of Jay Palmore. The intended use of the data was for policy purposes by NFPB, economic planning agencies, and academic institutions, to include the State of Michigan as well as University of Malaya, and apparently there was little consultation with these local institutions.

The NFPB, as the principal host of the project, had been sidelined in consultation regarding the use of the survey for planning and policy purposes. For instance, the University of Malaya, a top institution of higher education, employed a well-known local Professor of Statistics, Saw See Hok, who later told me he would have enjoyed being involved indirectly. Even if these people did not contribute in substantive and technical terms, they should have been informed and briefed about the content and progress of the survey, thereby giving them a sense of involvement.

As an American academic with little experience in the practical world, especially with governments in Asia embedded in their own bureaucratic cultures, Jay was technically competent, but not cognizant of the cultural milieu of the Malaysian setting in which he was doing his work. I have in the past frequently characterized this difference in attitude and behavior as "Americans with Baptist missionary zeal and Asians with cultural chauvinism."

In dealing with this Michigan predicament, I had to develop a workable rapport with the Director and then approach him with an argument that the survey data, with all the commensurate investment, could not be locked out unused, implying a tremendous waste of resources. I proposed that I start with a small pilot analysis of the survey data to illustrate and demonstrate the value of the survey for the NFPD and its reputation domestically and internationally. Poor Jay, after all the hard work he had done on an excellent survey, was shut out from using the data. For the initial paper using the survey data, I involved both sides as co-authors, Michigan and Malaysia, for publication, and this proved to be the key to resolving the Michigan predicament. Subsequently, Michigan was able to publish a remarkable volume on the Malaysian Fertility Survey in collaboration with NFPB. Later, Ron Freedman, the "god of fertility," wrote me a letter in which he said: "I am eternally grateful to you for what you have done . . ."[3]

In Malaysia, at the Department of Statistics in the Office of the Prime Minister, Chief Statistician Ramesh Chander, a wonderful colleague, arranged for me to work with the Demography Division with a staff of about thirty, including a number of statistical clerks also mobilized to conduct the Malaysian Fertility Survey with support from the Ford Foundation. In the absence of modern computers, my work on OCM applications and experiments was facilitated by the human resources available at the Department of Statistics.

I remember Bert Hoselitz, founder of the *Journal of Economic Development and Cultural Change* at Chicago, for his work on the sociological aspect of economic development. Post WWII UN development advisors recommended it to some developing countries. It involved the transfer of some tangible parts of the infrastructure of an economically advanced society—post office boxes, for example—with the idea being that what worked in America would work in underdeveloped Korea in the early stages of economic development. Therefore, Korea was given some steel post boxes!

I would like to cite a concrete example of American technical advice on the plan for the 1960 decennial census. During the planning stage, Mr. Lawrence, a respectable career Health, Education and Welfare civil servant and the census advisor of the Statistical Advisory Group, recommended the inclusion of a simple question on age in the census form: "How old are you?" As was the practice in past censuses in

---

3. An intriguing piece of the survey data was about a Malay woman in her late thirties with a history of seventeen marriages and divorces, and who, at the time of the survey, was remarried to her fourth husband. The Islamic custom of allowing a man to have four wives was practiced in Malaysia, and it was rapidly disappearing, but the cultural inertia was still in force for this woman.

the US, the question served as a direct transfer of the American way of getting age data instead of obtaining dates of birth, as was the practice in the Japanese colonial period, which had generated fairly accurate age data.

When counting age in East Asia, in the Chinese Cultural Sphere, there were two overlapping calendars used at the time: Western and Lunar. They were not synchronized. For example, a boy born on December 31 would be considered one year old at birth based on the tradition (*kazoetoshi* in Japan and *senunnai* in Korea) and then, on the next day in the new year (January 1) the boy would be two years old. The 1960 census was tabulated by the age of the population, and the results showed zero in the category of those less than one year of age. Even with the age data based on the dates of birth, there were underlying complications caused by the responses that used the Lunar or Western calendar, and referenced the "12-year animal year cycle." The Bureau of Statistics for the 1966 quinquennial census (delayed by one year) incorporated my recommendation for asking the date of birth in the Western or Lunar calendar, as well as indicating the "animal year."

The age data had to be adjusted and corrected to be useful in relation to the data collected on numerous characteristics and variables in the census as well as in the annual time series of the age data. The preliminary adjustments were performed to meet immediate requirements, but years later this became an academically challenging and demographically fascinating topic involving a leading economic demographer, Ansley Coale of Princeton, and myself.

Ansley was concurrently chairman of the U.S. National Academy Committee on Population and Demography established in 1977, composed of prominent demographers such as Bill Brass of the UK and others, and I was honored to be included as one of the two youngest members of the Committee along with Sam Preston of the University of Pennsylvania. My collaborative research with Ansley Coale was published in the *Report No.1, Estimation of Recent*

Trends in Fertility and Mortality in the Republic of Korea in the Academy's *NRC Report* series in 1980.

During my Malaysian assignment, I was requested by the Ford Foundation to provide some technical advice to the Indonesian Central Bureau of Statistics (BPS) where I became acquainted with Director General Abdul Mahjid and his competent professional staff. Sam Suharto and Si Gde Mamas later produced a monograph on the analysis of fertility based on the OCM application for Indonesia, involving Professor Kobayashi Kazumasa of Kyoto University. During my visit to Jakarta, I was requested to interview some candidates for scholarships supported by USAID to study in an American University, possibly at Chicago. The applicants were graduates of the professional school attached to the Central Bureau of Statistics. Among the four applicants, I found a bright young man, Hariyono Suyono, who later came to Chicago as a student and worked as one of my research assistants. (More later on his meteoric rise in Indonesia after his PhD.)

Sam Suharto of Indonesia (right, circa 1970s)

Having experienced a disastrous racial riot in Malaysia and an incident of mugging and injury in Chicago, I realized that ethnic and racial riots and tensions were historically a common denominator in cities with multiethnic populations. Certainly, the US was not excluded. In Malaysia, I enjoyed and shared some time together with Yuzuru (John) Takeshita, a sociologist from Michigan and former student of Ron Freedman who had worked with him on Taiwanese family planning studies. Takeshita was interned in California during WWII and in the later years of his career decided to be called by his Japanese name "Yuzuru" instead of John. However, he made an exception for me, saying "we were trusted and understanding friends." He also confided to me that his son was harassed by his peers in secondary school about his family name *Take-shit-a*, and in his adult age, committed suicide.

John Takeshita told me that at the time Hawai'i became the 50th State, Presidents Kennedy and Johnson worked out a major educational program with Senator Inouye establishing the East-West Center on the campus of the University of Hawai'i. He facilitated my communication with Hawai'i, which he stressed was an exceptional "harmonious multiethnic community." On my follow up visit to Honolulu, I was met at the airport by a friend of John's, Professor Douglas Yamamura of the Department of Sociology, later Chancellor of the University of Hawai'i at Mānoa. The first thing he did was drive me to a house on a ridge that was for sale. At the time I had other things on my mind as a priority. In retrospect, Doug Yamamura was right—I did not take his suggestion and missed the first real estate boom in Hawai'i.

19

THE EAST-WEST CENTER

"Where Wise Men of East and West Will Meet"

The East-West Center was established by the U.S. Congress in 1960 to promote better relations and understanding among the people and nations of the United States, Asia, and the Pacific through cooperative study, research, and dialogue, and to serve as the forum where "wise men of East and West will meet." In the late 1960s, under the direction of the Center's President Everett Kleinjans, the Center was restructured toward problem-oriented programs of mutual consequence in East and West and the global population issue affecting the Asia-Pacific region was the basis for the first such program through the establishment of the East-West Population Institute (EWPI).

An international advisory committee for the population program headed by Professor Phillip Hauser of Chicago included prominent demographers such as Ronald Freedman. The first director of the Institute was Paul Demeny who left his tenured professorship in the Economics Department at Michigan for Hawai'i and was a student of Ansley Coale's at Princeton. After a couple of years Paul left Hawai'i to take on the challenging work of developing a prestigious new journal for population and development (DPR) at the Population Council.

Dr. Everett Klenjans (Former President of East-West Center, circa late 1970s)

The East-West Center, with ample federal budgetary support, was recruiting young talent nationwide and I happened to fit into the scheme.

In 1970, after the completion and publication of my monograph, *Differential Current Fertility in the United States* (with assistance on the computation side from Professor Bogue's spouse Elizabeth Bogue and Hariyono Suyono of Indonesia), I moved to Hawai'i from Chicago to a joint appointment by the University of Hawai'i and the East-West Center's Population Institute (EWPI). It was one year after I had postponed the initial offer from Hawai'i.

Looking toward my future at the time, Hawai'i was an ideal and central geographical location for doing work in Asia and the U.S. mainland, with a relaxed social environment in harmony with ethnic affinity. At the East-West Center, I was most impressed with a group of bright young researchers the EWPI was able to recruit, including Robert Retherford, Griffith Feeney, and W. Brian Arthur; fresh PhDs from Berkeley; as well as Fred Arnold from Harvard, Jay Palmore from Michigan, Geoffery McNicoll from Australian National University (ANU), and others. Brian Arthur, an Irish national from Northern Ireland later accepted an offer from Stanford for a chaired professorship, but a few years later left Stanford to join a research institution doing innovative work, telling me "Teaching at Stanford was boring."

One of the first projects I started at East-West Population Institute (EWPI) in 1972 was the Census and Statistics Directors' Meeting for Asia, which was later expanded to the Pacific and Americas as the Association of National Census and Statistics Directors of Asia, America and the Pacific (ANCSDAP). Most of the countries, starting with the US Census Bureau, China's Central Statistical Office, and Japan's Bureau of Statistics, were consistent participants as well as hosts of the conference series.

The OCM (Own Children Method) applications to the 1966 Census and 1970 Census of Korea were done as a joint project of BOS Korea and EWPI. I was really grateful to Bill Brass for his suggestion of incorporating into the OCM his technique for estimating childhood mortality based on the survival of children born, which he believed would have great potential. This was similar to what was done in the 1974 publication by Yonsei University Press of the own children estimates for Korea. Brass noted Griffith Feeney's contribution to the solution of "the problem of relating the proportion of children who had died classified by the age of the mother to time trends in child mortality." The applications of the OCM for estimating fertility were rapidly extended to most of the countries in Southeast Asia starting with Malaysia and Indonesia.

In 1974, I was appointed as Director of the EWPI while concurrently maintaining a full professorship with the University of Hawai'i, and when the East-West Center was subsequently incorporated as an independent educational institution with its own Board of Governors, I chose the Center as my home base and became an adjunct with the University.

In the post-WWII and Korean War years, mainland China became a black hole in terms of its population and demography. Any information about its population was welcomed, with its very high scarcity value. In Hong Kong during that time, there were some experts making speculations about some basic parameters of the mainland population on the basis of interviews with migrants from China.

The demographers at the Princeton Office of Population Research, George Barclay and Ansley Coale, in consultation with Alexander Eckstein of the University of Michigan (the leading China economist at the time) whom I was happy to meet at Ann Arbor, were searching for the whereabouts of Tuan Chihsien. Chihsien had assisted Barclay in an earlier Taiwan project (*Colonial Development and Population in Taiwan*), and then came to study at Princeton in the early 1950s. A year and half later, he left for the London School of Economics to stay for about eight months and then disappeared. Around 1975, Coale and Eckstein approached me to help search for Tuan and told me the U.S. Department of State was cooperating in this endeavor. Tuan, when found, could be a valuable resource for potentially developing a leading program for Chinese demography at the EWPI. A couple of years later, in a roundabout way, we were pleasantly surprised to find Tuan Chihsien not in Mainland China, but in Hong Kong.

As a young intellectual, Tuan, originally from the Mainland, returned to China to work for the Communist Revolution. With the development of his motherland in his professional field of agricultural development, and his educational background and experience in rural development in Taiwan, he was assigned to a researcher's position at the Chinese Academy of Agriculture.

With Tuan Chihsien (circa 1980s)

Afterward, he was transferred to the Beijing Normal School on the basis of his English proficiency, where he suffered harassment by students participating in the Cultural Revolution. His offense was having some change in U.S. dollars, and coins and letters in English from outside of China. In the 1950s, numerous young Chinese in the countries of Southeast Asia, in particular, Indonesia, came to take part in the Revolution of their fatherland, and one of them was a young woman whom Tuan married and who later gave birth to their daughter, Jasmine.

During the later phase of the Cultural Revolution, Tuan was deported to a remote village commune and suffered a miserable condition of life while his wife was sent to another rural location. It is said: "Disaster sometimes brings some blessing." The Chinese government at the time made an exception in the treatment of those who came from outside China like Mrs. Tuan, and gave them the choice to return to their country of origin. Tuan benefitted from his spouse's identity and was able to exit the China Mainland with his family to arrive in Hong Kong on Christmas day in 1973.

He survived in Hong Kong doing some English teaching and translation work, and when we located him, he was extremely pleased about our search and eagerly looking forward to joining us in Hawai'i. Snags develop when bigger things are going well. In applying for an entry visa to the US on a non-immigrant exchange status, during the interview at the U.S. Consulate in answer to a question on his intention after the exchange program, he gave his honest answer: he wanted to stay in the US permanently. This changed his visa situation drastically, initiating a four-to-five-year delay in the issuance of an immigrant visa. Finally, he was granted a permanent visa to arrive in Hawai'i in 1980. Tuan said later it took longer to get out of Hong Kong than going through the arduous process to exit Mainland China.

During his long wait for a visa in Hong Kong, we had assigned Tuan to do whatever work he could to evaluate the work of others speculating on China and to translate whatever was relevant to Chinese population policy. We were gearing up for the development of our China Population program with the Population Institute in consultation with Coale and Eckstein.

After his arrival, Tuan wrote a comprehensive essay on the demographic situation of the People's Republic of China and developed an institutional road map for future research cooperation with China. He made indispensable and invaluable contributions in opening and developing successful cooperative arrangements with the major government institutions in China relevant to population policy and data. The EWPI enjoyed having the leading edge on population study in China. As the saying goes: "All roads lead to Rome," and prominent junior and senior demographers with interest in China wanted to come to us.

Ansley Coale and his Princeton colleagues, Ron Freedman of Michigan, Sidney Goldstein of Brown and other prominent academics, on one hand, and junior demographers like Judith Banister (who, after her stint with us, joined the U.S. Census Bureau as the leading China expert) and Susan Greenhalgh on the other, came to join us. Susan first started as an intern with her interest in the anthropology of Chinese demography, but later joined Harvard as a professor, and then became the John King and Wilma Cannon Fairbank Research Professor of Chinese Society, Emerita, in the Department of Anthropology at Harvard University.

As for the China Demography Project of EWPI, we were the first to develop a uniquely close working relationship with the People's Republic of China, especially with the Planned Births Commission and the Central Bureau of Statistics, and we were grateful to our friends and partners in China. We were really fortunate, in this unique cooperative arrangement, to be given access to the 1987 survey data and a one per thousand sample of the Chinese Censuses of 1990 and 2000. I continued to cooperate with some of their younger generations in related areas.

Using that 1987 one percent population survey, Griffith Feeney, Feng Wang, Mingkun Zhou, and Baoyu Xiao did the analysis of the first detailed national-level data since the 1982 census, also using the OCM extension to parity progression data.[1]

The analysis of fertility trends derived by applying the own-children method of fertility estimation to China's 1990 and 2000 censuses by Robert D. Retherford, Minja Kim Choe, Jiajian Chen et al. was published in March 2005 in *Population and Development Review.*

Earlier, Griff Feeney and Yu Jingyuan, a leading system scientist in China, worked together on the parity

1. *Population and Development Review (PDR)* 15, no. 2 (June 1989), pp. 297–322.

progression analysis for China at EWPI. Yu is one of my lifetime professional colleagues and friends, along with Song Jian, former Chairman and Vice Premier of the Science and Technology Commission (SSTC), who came to EWPI on several occasions and is currently honorary president of the Chinese Academy of Engineering.

In 1996, Bill Brass, in my estimation the international authority on incomplete data, published an article in *Population Studies* called "Demographic Data Analysis in Less Developed Countries:1946–1996," in which he featured OCM, concluding: "During the past twenty-five years 'the own children method' has been increasingly refined. It extends the reverse survival strategy, primarily to produce more detailed measures of fertility, but also in some respects to improve accuracy." The methodology later proved to have a remarkable potential in the estimation of differential fertility and historical demography.

David A. Coleman, Professor and Director of the Population Studies Center of the University of Oxford, wrote me a letter requesting permission and cooperation in the use of OCM in a major project for "Estimating Fertility by Ethnic and Religious Groups in the UK, 1960s–2006," supported by the British government. Coleman and Sylvie Dubuc published the results in *Population Studies*, Vol. 64, No. 1, 2010.

Research continued, and years afterwards, an international conference on "Children, Mothers and Measuring Fertility: New Perspectives on the Own Child Method" was co-hosted by the Universities of Cambridge and Essex at the Geography Department, University of Cambridge from September 18 to 20, 2017.[2] The conference announcement stated, "Grabill and Cho's Own Child Method (OCM), for calculating fertility measures from individual level census data or

2. The conference proceedings were published as *Demography of Incomplete Data: Own Child Methodology, Past and Present* (Northeast Asia Economic Forum and College of Social Sciences, University of Hawai'i at Mānoa, 2021).

similar sources, has seen something of a resurgence in recent years. Practitioners have been using the method in both historical and present-day contexts."

At this meeting, members of the team from the Universities of Cambridge and Essex presented their findings alongside other scholars with a wealth of experience in the use of OCM. The meeting provided an opportunity to compare and contrast findings, discuss the advantages and pitfalls of the method, and explore the understanding it offers for fertility and fertility-related behavior in a variety of temporal and spatial settings.

An email message from Peter McDonald about the applications of OCM by Australian National University (ANU) read as follows, "Jalal Abbasi-Shavazi won the United Nations Population Award, with the following citation: 'Our main publication in the Iran work is the book by Abbasi-Shavazi, M. J., McDonald, P. and Hosseini-Chavoshi, M. in 2009, *The Fertility Transition in Iran: Revolution and Reproduction,* and a journal article by McDonald, P., Hosseini-Chavoshi, M., Abbasi-Shavazi, M. and Rashidian, A. in 2015, containing "An assessment of recent Iranian fertility trends using parity progression ratios." *Demographic Research* 32 (Article 58): 1581–1602." McDonald's email concluded, "Looks like we get all of our methods from EWPI." In the earlier period of my Institute Directorship, some colleagues referred to it as "East-West Own Children Institute."

"The center of the population and demographic research [is] shifting toward Hawai'i," wrote Karen Mason, Professor of Sociology at Michigan and past president of the Population Association of America, who left a tenured position of full professor to join the EWPI. Ron Freedman told me Michigan was losing her. Nathan Keyfitz, my dissertation committee member (who later moved to Berkeley) joined us as EWPI Senior Fellow with a joint appointment to the

University of Hawai'i. Our Institute was rated as one of the top research centers for two decades. Nathan later left us for Harvard and retired as emeritus and Karen joined the World Bank as director of its gender department.

In my last letter to Professor Nathan Keyfitz, I wrote:

> Dear Nathan,
>
> Your card of December 22, 2006, finally reached me and I was very pleased to read your thoughtful note, and Pushkin's poem "Work." I remember several years ago we happened to see each other while I was having dinner with my historian friend Carter Eckert at the Club House on the Harvard Campus. Nathan, you were a brilliant and truly stimulating teacher, and opened my horizon into new dimensions of demography. Your contributions during your stay with us at the East-West Center Population Institute prior to your joining Harvard were really valuable and memorable . . . I have always been greatly appreciative of the fact that I had a great teacher like you and of your friendship. Please convey my best regards to Beatrice.
>
> Cordially,
> Lee-Jay and Eun-Ja Cho

I am truly indebted to my colleagues who worked as a team to extend and refine the Own Children Methodology. They include Robert Retherford, Griffith Feeney, Norman Luther and Minja Kim Choe.

Robert Retherford, emeritus Senior Fellow and former Director of the Population Studies Program at the East-West Center, was one of the most brilliant and innovative demographers who joined the EWPI, with a BA and a PhD from Berkeley. He contributed greatly to the extensions and applications of the OCM and was offered a professorship at Harvard University. Bob went to Cambridge to visit the campus, but called me to say he declined the offer and would be returning to the EWPI to continue working on our creative collaborative work.

Griffith Feeney, emeritus Senior Fellow at EWPI and a brilliant demographer, joined the Institute at a young age, with a BA from the University of Michigan and a PhD from Berkeley. Griffith Feeney did much to extend, apply, and refine the methodology. For example, his notes for instruction and training for the method have been widely used internationally. Griff declined a professorship from Brown University to continue his research with us. Brian Arthur later moved to Stanford University.

Minja Kim Choe, whom I met at Chicago when she was starting graduate work for an MA in mathematics, followed her husband to Cambridge for his PhD dissertation and worked as a senior computer programmer at an MIT physics laboratory. She contributed substantially to the configuration of the OCM computer software package.

Norman Luther, in his presentation on "*Personal Reminiscences and Norman Luther's Own Children Method Bibliography*"[3] at the most recent conference at the East-West Center in 2017, provided a fascinating anecdote about his introduction to demography:

> I'm pretty unusual in my background as to how I came to this place. I was trained as a mathematician and spent the beginning of my career at Washington State University. I was actually a theoretical mathematician, but I always had an interest in social science applications. At the time the math department at

3. This presentation was published in whole in *Festschrift in Memory of Professor Donald J Bogue of the University of Chicago* (Yonsei University Press, 2020).

Washington State University got a small grant, I think from the National Science Foundation, to encourage the pursuit of so-called interdisciplinary options. I went on sabbatical to the Population Institute at the East-West Center to study and do research in mathematical demography. I started at the bottom there, as an intern on sabbatical, under the original sponsorship of the late Jay Palmore. I ended up doing more work with other people. Robert (Bob) Retherford was one of them. I worked on fitting fertility age distributions with mathematical functions which later became one of the components of the birth history reconstruction procedure, otherwise known as the extended own children method. When I later went back to the East-West Center, Lee-Jay Cho presented me with the following question. Given census or survey data with incomplete birth histories of women containing the ages of those in the household but not of those deceased children nor surviving children not in the household (called "non-own children")—ordinarily giving them numbers, the women's numbers—is it possible to reconstruct (in other words, complete) the birth histories by somehow imputing the age of the deceased and non-own children? The second entry in the bibliography I provide here is the seminal paper that gives the original birth history reconstruction procedure. This is the paper produced with Lee-Jay Cho: "Reconstruction of birth histories from census and household survey data," 1988, *Population Studies*, 42(3):451–472.

For example, because of the one child family policy, China was very interested in using the procedure particularly for calculating the proportion of women progressing from first to second birth. Several workshops, both here and in China, were scheduled by and for the Chinese, including one in China to which Griffith (Griff) Feeney and I were invited to introduce the procedure and accompanying parity progression ratios to participants from all over China.

This trip to China was very interesting. I was never treated so well in my life. First of all, members of our family (Griff's and mine) were invited to come along and go on a side trip after the workshop was over. Griff brought his dad, his wife, and their two very young children and I brought my wife and sister-in-law.

After the workshop, they took us all into Huangshan which is a revered area of China where ethnic Chinese come back from other countries to visit. We were there for two or three days and we saw only one other American the whole time. He was a geologist from the University of Montana because this area is of geological interest. Our guide for this trip was a lady who was participating in the summer seminar and was also in charge of the logistics for our workshop. Interestingly, she is now a faculty member at the University of South Carolina and we are still in touch with her. Anyway, we heard that this was the first time that the authorities in China had let participants eat lunch with those from the US conducting workshops. The entries (works) on the original birth history reconstruction procedure had a great deal of influence from Lee-Jay Cho, of course. I have two significant remarks. Griff said that the application of the birth history reconstruction procedure described in this paper allowed him to know more about Chinese fertility than anybody else at that time (1990). Secondly, Bill Lavely of the University of Washington told me that he used this paper as a model article for his classes (note the reference to William Lavely, James

Lee, and Wang Feng, 1990, "Chinese demography: The state of the field," *The Journal of Asian Studies*, 49(4):807–834.

Curiously, I found at home the Chinese edition of the comprehensive work entitled "The own-children method of fertility estimation." I have an English version too, *The Own Children Method of Fertility Estimation*, 1996, Chinese Edition. Beijing: Science Press. (With Lee-Jay Cho, Robert D. Retherford, and Minja Choe.)

The last thing I want to mention is the Korean-American connection. This is something very personal and dear to my heart that brought this work into focus again. It happened some 45 years after my late father, Dr. Chester F. Luther, retired in 1972 as head of the Mathematics Department at Willamette University in Salem, Oregon, where I grew up before attending undergraduate study at Stanford University and doctoral study in math at the University of Iowa. One of his last students donated a large sum of money to fund an endowed professorship chair in my father's name. This person, who had gone on to become an executive at Boeing, credited his success to my father encouraging him to finish his two years at Columbia University in the joint engineering program with Willamette University that my father had helped to set up. Following the celebration of this gift to the university, I discussed the birth history reconstruction procedure with the present Chair of the Mathematics Department at Willamette University. He was the first occupant of the endowed chair in my father's name. He was quite interested in the procedure because it brings mathematics to real life. It turned out that he was a native Korean who had been adopted by a single mother in New Hampshire.

> And so this Korean-American connection continues, having started with my co-author in the seminal birth history reconstruction procedure paper, Lee-Jay Cho, a Korean-American. Others to also be thanked once again in closing are Bob Retherford and Griff Feeney as primary users of my procedure and Minja Choe, a primary pioneer in encouraging international scholars to adopt its use and, incidentally, a Korean-American.

In the course of dynamic developments and accomplishments, the EWPI was gradually gaining recognition and reputation both in the US and internationally, and thus, Professor Hauser enjoyed serving as chairman of the Institute Advisory committee. Phil was generous and used to take many of us and our staff for lunch or dinner and told many fun jokes, which were very entertaining. I still remember his anecdotal quips about past U.S. Presidents: "Franklin Roosevelt proved a patrician can be President; Harry Truman proved a farmer can be a (good) president (he worked for Truman); Dwight Eisenhower proved you don't need a President; Richard Nixon proved a crook can be president; Ronald Reagan proved an actor can be president." I don't know what he would say about Trump, if he were still living, and I would guess something like "a crazy moron . . . ."

Phil was also sociable and gracious to people around him, and I still remember him picking up Nuy, my baby daughter, saying "ding dong ding" every time we got together with his kind-hearted wife Zelda, a cousin of Maestro Silverstein of the Boston Pops Orchestra.

20

PERSONAL AND INSTITUTIONAL TIES TO JAPAN

In the early 1980s, I assisted Dr. Kuroda Toshio, after his term as Director of Population Institute of the Ministry of Welfare, in the establishment of NUPRI and the EWPI, having maintained a close cooperative relationship with him for many years. Phil Hauser and I played the advisory role in strengthening NUPRI and it became the top population research center in Japan.

With Nobutsuke Kishi (former Prime Minister of Japan) to my right and Dr. Kuroda Toshio, second from right (circa early 1980s)

At the request of Dr. Kuroda, founding director of NUPRI, the EWPI sent him one of our most outstanding students, Ogawa Hiro, who later became the leading demographer in Japan. Some years later Phil Hauser recommended Tsuya Noriko, who moved to Keio University, where she currently has the title of Distinguished Professor. I had several of our able researchers, for example, Bob Retherford and Linda Martin, one of my assistant directors who took a special interest in Sumo (grand champion Kitanoumi) and tofu, work in Tokyo with NUPRI.

Kuroda-sensei (professor) and I maintained a long and productive professional and personal relationship dating back to the early 1960s. The later phase in our cooperative relationship with Nihon University resulted in its upgrade to a direct report to the office of the President and the establishment of the University Research Center (URC) on my suggestion. This created a much broader framework for population studies in Japan involving cross- and interdisciplinary collaborations with relevant parts of different schools and colleges. As an example, Kuroda-sensei and I were involved in the topic of demographic and industrial transition in the context of the idea of the "Pan-Pacific Community" of Professor Kojima Kiyoshi, fellow alumnus of Tokyo College of Commerce, which now is Hitotsubashi University.

We, the Kuroda and Cho families, also share some fascinating and painful histories going back to the sixteenth-century invasion of Korea by Toyotomi Hideyoshi. Kuroda-sensei was a direct descendant of Kuroda Kanbei, second only to Hideyoshi as chief counselor with his own *Han,* a fiefdom based in the Himeji (Castle) where he was from and where he had his estate. In Fukuoka, Kyushu, Kanbei's son was Nagamasa, another historical figure who inherited the title of Daimyo at the age of 27 from his father Kanbei.

With my in-laws, Dr. and Mrs. Kuroda, and Mr. and Mrs. Nishiyama (circa 1990s)

Kuroda Kanbei and his son, Nagamasa, joined the invading Japanese forces and landed in Busan with the fearsome Kato Kiyomasa and Nabeshima Naoshige, who were ancestors to Kuroda-sensei's wife. A combined force of some 27,000, they marched west on foot to Chinju to awesome *Jiri Mountain,* a steep and high, rough natural barrier with a fortress, *Hwangseok Sansung,* designated as a historic site. Blocking the entire narrow pathway to *Namwon,* they went beyond the mountain leading to Seoul, the capital of *Joseon* (Korea).

As an aside, *Namwon* is the original hometown of the famous *Satsuma Yaki* Porcelain of Kagoshima, originated by Shim Soo Kwan, winner of the first prize at the Paris International Exhibition at the turn of the nineteenth Century.

The Korean Army was almost totally disintegrated with no leadership and some of the soldiers were even helping the invading Japanese in return for cash. But in the Korean channel in the south, Admiral Lee Soonshin, with his historic leadership and ingenuity in concocting Korea's armored warship or *Turtle Boat,* was managing to maintain Korea's naval superiority.

At the time, with the Korean Army in chaos, in the absence of any military forces to fight against the Japanese, the Korean intelligentsia organized groups of volunteer resistance guerrilla fighters. The ancestors of the Cho family were some of its prominent leaders, and one of them manned the *Hwangseok Sansung* fortress with some 3,500 volunteers, including many women who provided support with whatever they could find to fight (such as farm tools, rocks, and stones) to face down the well-equipped, numerically superior enemy. The Korean defendants fought tooth and nail and committed *gyokusai* in the same manner as the Japanese force's final suicidal defense of Saipan Island in the later phase of the Pacific War. The Kurodas and my family realize that history has strange turns and serendipitous outcomes. Mrs. Kuroda made an apologetic observation at the time: "Sad! My ancestors also participated in the tragedy of the Cho family."

There was a field trip on one occasion in the 1980s when Dr. Kuroda and I were accompanied by some close Cho family descendants to visit the historic site at Jirisan. We returned in the evening to a dinner commemorating this historic event going back 400 years, as well as the peace and friendship between the Kuroda and Cho lines. At the dinner, Dr. Kuroda remarked: "It was very hard to understand why my ancestors wore about eighteen pairs of *warajin* (rice straw sandals, as he estimated) for the seventeen-day march on foot from Busan to Jirisan . . . ."

Historians have given credit to Kuroda Kanbei for his anti-war efforts and his critical role in withdrawing the invading troops from Korea and attempting to save Sen no Rikyū, for opposing the Korean Invasion at the risk of his life, as one version of an NHK Tiger drama series about Kuroda

Kanbei that I watched portrayed it. Sen no Rikyū incidentally, is the founder of the Japanese "way" of tea ceremony. Joseon Monthly Magazine published an article about the Kuroda/Cho story with the photo of the two of us shaking hands at the battle site, portraying close friends whose ancestors fought as enemies four centuries ago.

The success of the Nihon University Population Institute (NUPRI) would not have been possible without the support and dedication of an able administrator and manager for academic and research programs in the Japanese university setting, Mr. Kawarazaki Fukuji, who fulfilled this indispensable role for NUPRI and Director Kuroda. The three of us had an especially close bond in both working and personal relationships.

Kawarazaki-san, as we used to call him affectionately, was physically short, less than five feet in stature, but he was seven feet tall in trust and loyalty. He was close to being a workaholic, spending most of his time at the office by staying on the fourth floor of the building where NUPRI was located at the College of Economics at Chinbo-cho, except on weekends. Around that time in the 1980s, there was a Chinese student, Wang Shenjin (Oh Shyokon in Japanese), studying at Nihon University with partial support from NUPRI. Kawarazaki invited him to share a room on the fourth floor, helping out with Wang's lodging expenses.

Kuroda regarded and treated Wang like his student and son, and Wang always considered Kuroda as his parent and me a mentor and teacher. Although Professor Kuroda has long since passed away, our relationship continued. At my last meeting with Wang Shenjin in Changchun, knowing that I was planning to see Kawarazaki-san bedridden in a hospital, Wang asked me to convey his best wishes for a fast recovery and told me to relay to Kawarazaki-san what he felt was his unforgettable teaching tenet in administration and management: "Confirm, confirm, and confirm."

Mr. Fukuji Kawarazaki (left) and Dr. Toshio Kuroda (right, 2006)

My wife and I went to Nagano and found Kawarazaki-san on a hospital bed, unconscious in the presence of his wife and family. They told us he had been unconscious for several days. I spoke to him in a large voice, holding his hands, greeting him "Kawarazaki-san . . ." and he responded by gripping my hands a bit. When I conveyed the message from Wang, or *Oh Shyokon,* and asked him about his bank account with the Bank of Hawaii (my wife and I helped him maintain this account by having the statements mailed to our home address), he tried to open his eyes and responded by gripping my hand stronger and moving his legs. This was felt and noticed by his wife and son and my wife, who were watching by his side.

His doctor confirmed that I had communicated with Kawarazaki-san, and his family was so pleased. I told Mrs. Kawarazaki that when the value of the Japanese yen was extraordinarily high in the 1980s, I had suggested her husband buy U.S. dollars at an exchange rate roughly in the range of

50–60 yen per dollar. He then purchased the U.S. dollars and deposited the funds into his account at the Bank of Hawaii, saying: "This is for the trip to Hawai'i with my wife after retirement." Mrs. Kawarazaki, sobbing, responded: "He never told me about this." The story reaffirmed her husband's love and care for her. Kawarazaki-san passed away a couple of weeks afterward, and I was able to transfer a balance of $10,000 USD to Mrs. Kawarazaki, who confirmed the receipt of what she felt was the most valuable gift of love from her husband.

For the funeral, I sent my eulogy poem in Kanji, starting with "*Kakunin* (confirm), *kakunin, kakunin. . . .*", a tribute to Kawarazaki-san for turning NUPRI into the leading population research center in Japan.

I later found out that Wang mastered Japanese by learning and practicing the Japanese *Enka* song, verses of which are beautiful and poetic and by participating in popular Japanese song contests, known as *utagassen* (Korean *norejarang*). He eventually won an envied championship competition singing "*Subaru,* the stars." With his fluent Japanese and his academic ability, he became one of the leading scholars on Japan Sea Rim economic cooperation, as seen from the Chinese perspective. He was the founding dean of the Center for Southeast Asian Studies, and subsequently was appointed Executive Vice President of Jilin University, one of the largest major universities in China, where he is currently Lifetime Special University professor.

Kawarazaki, thanks to his extraordinary performance, recognized by the leaders of the University, went through several steps of promotion to hold his final position as Secretary General for the University Research Center (URC). He arranged an internship for my daughter Nuy as an undergraduate student at URC (an "Introduction to Japanese Culture 101" in practice) and found a suitable home stay for her in Sugamo. At Nuy's host home, following the

Japanese tradition, she was asked to enter the house not from the main front door but from the rear entrance like other female members of the family. This was a cultural shock to her, having grown up in an American cultural and educational environment.

Sugamo Penitentiary is where Japanese war criminals like Tojo Hideki of WWII were jailed, along with others including Tōgō Shigenori, a descendant of Korean ceramic artisans kidnapped and brought to Japan in Namwon beyond Jirisan in Southern Korea (more about this later.) Foreign Minister Shigenori declared war with the United States in 1941 and a few years later, in 1945, he returned to the same position to consent to Japan's unconditional surrender on behalf of the War Tribunal. Only a short distance away is *Yasukuni Jinja,* near the main campus of Nihon University, where the Japanese paid tribute and respect to their war heroes. It was my favorite jogging ground.

In 1980, after spending three months with my wife, five-year-old daughter Nuy, and baby boy Ray, in a rented house arranged by Kawarazaki-san in Nakano, Tokyo (I was working with Nihon University), we moved to Kyoto at the invitation of Director Ichimura Shinichi at the Kyoto University Center for Southeast Asian Studies. I was invited as a visiting scholar. We settled in a nice house surrounded by rice paddies at Iwakura only a few miles north from the Kyoto University campus. This was arranged by Dr. Tsubouchi, whom I met in Malaysia in 1968 during his field trip for his doctoral dissertation in sociology.

Our lodging was his second house, and we paid a nominal, discounted rent. The Tsubouchis lived in a house near the rail track with his mother, who was in her seventies. They were extremely nice and helpful to us in many ways. On weekdays, I commuted to the Center on a local bus and interacted with the faculty members, starting with Professor Ichimura, an economist; Kobayashi, an anthropologist;

Yasuba, an economist; and others in agriculture, political science, and history. For me, the opportunity in Kyoto was an ideal occasion for spending time with family and relatives in the Kansai area while at the same time pursuing different interests.

I engaged a student well-versed in Japanese literature for individual lessons on the works of Natsume Soseki and others and learned a lot from her. During this time, I felt a strong urge to improve my Mandarin pronunciation, memorizing the structure of the wording. I went to a large bookstore in Kyogoku, a central shopping mall, to find that the only available item was a set of cassette tapes for beginners with a companion text that turned out to be a collection of Chairman Mao's speeches, selected from the *Red Book* produced during the Cultural Revolution by the Central Beijing Broadcasting Company. I studied the text and listened to the tapes during my jogging and walking for a number of years, and I was able to recite a few important parts of Mao's speeches. Years later, audiences on the Chinese mainland appreciated the quotations in my speeches in Chinese.

So that she could socialize and interact with the Japanese children, I took Nuy on Sundays to Heian Kyokai, the church kindergarten, on a bike. One morning, my daughter was sitting behind me with her arms around my waist, when she accidentally stuck her feet in the rear wheel spikes, resulting in a bloody and painful injury to her feet. With some friendly help, we were able to see a doctor, who happened to be Korean, at Kyoto University Hospital. He kindly treated the wounds and Nuy recovered shortly afterwards. She enjoyed kindergarten, was popular, and was given a jolly farewell party by her classmates and their parents.

At Kyoto University, I worked with Professor Kobayashi, an anthropologist and demographer specializing in migration and a graduate of Tokyo University in anthropology and anatomy as was required by the medical school.

Kobayashi referred me to his co-authored paper, a study of historical migration from the Korean Peninsula with Hanihara Kazuro, a leading anthropologist and alumnus at Tokyo University, a few years behind—his *Kohai.* I was introduced to Professor Haniwara, who retired from Tokyo University to become Vice Director of the International Research Center for Japanese Studies in Kyoto. Having learned he did his post-doc at the University of Chicago, we enjoyed a fascinating dialogue about the *Toraijin* in Japan.

Hanihara's major works, published in the 1980s, were on geographic variation of modern Japanese crania, its relationship to the origin of the Japanese, and estimation of the number of early migrants to Japan. Historical Korean migration to Japan is seen as pivotal in the development of Japanese demography, culture, and tradition, and this is based on bio-anthropological, archaeological, linguistic, and historical studies.

As Jared Diamond argues in *Guns, Germs and Steel: The Fates of Human Societies* (1999), the history of human civilization provides us with ample evidence of technologically superior groups or nations that have conquered, dominated, or exterminated weaker ones. For example, the American continent was conquered by Europeans, and Australia by the British. In only rare cases were the weaker groups or nations left alone, although there were some exceptions largely due to natural and geographical barriers. Only in recent human history, in a temporally miniscule portion have we observed an institutionalization of respect for national sovereignty.

Korean migration can also be seen as an example of the "dissemination model," in which skills and technology are transferred through human contact and migration. Historians contend that Japan, for example, benefited from migrants from the Korean peninsula during a few centuries around the birth of Christ. These immigrants brought steel-making technology, organization and political management skills (the so-called Horserider Theory / *kiba minzoku kokkaron*), and political entities led by horse riders from the Asian continent, according to historian *Egami Namio*). Professor Egami was academically ostracized for going against the traditional historians' hold on the origin of the Japanese that is based on the mythological Amaterasu Omikami God.

The findings from the Hanihara study of historical migration from the Korean Peninsula are based on the measurements of a large number of sample skulls from tombs going back to the third century BC to span a thousand years up to the seventh century AD. These findings made a sensation in Japan as well as internationally, including in *The New York Times*. I asked Hanihara a personal question. Was he afraid of any threat of physical harm? He confidently stated his work was scientific and announced that anyone who differed and disagreed with him could come to him. He told me no one showed up.

Hanihara's scientific evidence showed that migrants from the continent, particularly from the Korean peninsula (*toraijin*), dominated northern Kyushu initially, gradually moving from the western part to Kansai and the Yamato plain and eventually concentrating in Nara, Kyoto, and Ohmi, the historic capitals of Japan. For Kyoto, the study showed 99 percent of the inhabitants historically were *Toraijin* and because of his sensational study, Professor Haniwara was given an audience with Emperor Hirohito. In front of the Emperor, Hanihara said: "His Majesty also is *Toraijin*" and the Emperor responded: "*Ah, sodeska,* is that so."

Toraijin introduced a new governing structure, along with continental culture and material technology and gradually advanced toward the east, overcoming the aborigines, who were not equipped to stop the superior advancing forces with steel weapons. It is argued that in recorded history, the ruling stratum in Japan was composed of migrants from the continent, including the imperial family, who in recent years have acknowledged its origin as *toraijin* from the Korean peninsula.

Hanihara's study of *Toraijin* in some important way was related to my interest in linguistic anthropology, corroborated by *The Origin of the Japanese Language,* a seminal work by Professor Ohno Susumu of Gakushuin University, a higher educational institution for nobility. I had a fascinating dialogue with Ohno in Tokyo.

Ohno, in his work, found the common structure and agglutination of the Korean and Japanese languages and the pattern of change in etymology of the basic and elementary vocabulary over time, most notably in Japanese since he was not well versed in Korean. He manifested his strong interest in the pursuit of this topic. Ohno and I enjoyed a very productive discussion in which we played a little game of transforming words over time in Japanese.

With my bilingual capability, I came to realize the Japanese language is an archaic Korean with variation over centuries. I felt more confident and at home with the Japanese language, unlike most people who understood it as having a separate and independent ancestry. Ohno and I agreed it would be a good idea for me to collect the words my mother spoke in her generation, coming from the Southern part of the Korean Peninsula where ancient migrants left for the Japanese archipelago. I wrote down a number of words from my mother that reinforced my interest in the bilingual comparison.

Some interesting examples are the Korean word *ip,* mouth, which the Japanese made a verb, *ipu,* which over time changed to *ifu* and then to its current form *iu,* meaning to speak out of mouth. The Korean word *ko,* nose, changed to the Japanese verb ***kogu*** and now is ***kagu,*** to smell with nose. On both sides "O" changed over time to the "A" sound in many other words. The word *ue,* above, is the same in both languages. *Nobda,* high in Korean, is the Japanese verb *noboru,* climbing high. *Padtaegi* in Southern Korea and *h(p) atake* in Japanese means a dried field for raising crops. The only rule of this change over time was that the sound "P" changed to "H." This applies to numerous other words in Japanese.

As mentioned, Kyoto and Nara were historically concentrated by *Toraijins*. I discovered some interesting remnants of the Kyoto vernacular used in the villages that are common with the Southern Korean dialect. The pattern of change from the "H" sound to "S" applies both in Korean and Japanese, and *suru,* in modern Japanese meaning "do," was *haru* in the long past. The Korean word for "do" is *handa*, and following agglutination, the past tense becomes *haetda* and correspondingly in Japanese *hatda*.

Once, a long time ago, when I revisited my birthplace of Terada Mura (village) and said "hello" to Takemura Akiko, the surviving daughter of our neighbor, who was very friendly to my parents, Aki-chan (as our family used to call her intimately) asked me: "*Ottosan sine hatda?*" Word by word, this is "Father death did" meaning "Did your father pass away?" Along the same pattern, Koreans would say *siksa haedta* meaning "meal (kanji word) did." And in Japanese, *shokuji* (the same kanji word) *hadta*. Right after our stay in Kyoto we were invited by Dong-A University to a short stay at their guest house in Dadaepo, by the seaside. My daughter Nuy, as a child with keen audio perception, made an observation: "In Kyoto, words for welcoming the guests at the entrance, *genkan,* sound almost the same in Korean, *oso oyso,* and *oide yasu* in Kyoto with the same tone (__ -_).

Of course, the majority of Japan's vocabulary was based on Chinese characters. Kanji (incorporated centuries later), essentially shared common meaning, as we group China, Korea and Japan into "the Chinese character cultural sphere," and the kanji words are fitted into the basic Ural Altaic linguistic structural frame to which Korean,

Mongolian, Manchurian, Hungarian, and Finnish belong.[1] There are two ways of reading kanji in Japan, namely: *on yomi* (approximating the original Chinese pronunciation) and *kun yomi* (a phonetic representation using kanji in the vernacular) practiced as *Yidu* during the Silla Dynasty in the seventh to tenth centuries in Korea. For example: "*jin*" (person) in *on yomi,* "*ren*" (in Chinese today), "*in*" in Korean and "*hito*" in Japanese *kun yomi.* I understood from my historian colleagues that back in the Tang Dynasty period in the seventh to tenth centuries, the literate population of the three countries were able to communicate with each other much better than they do today using the kanji and pildam (brush talk). This continental cultural and technological dissemination and influence continued until the opening of Japan in the nineteenth century.

A reference was made earlier to the incident during the Hideyoshi invasion of Korea in the sixteenth century, of the kidnapping of forty-seven families of ceramic artisans in Namwon to Japan. The ceramic culture and art of China and Korea along with anything of religious, philosophical, and literary content, were the envy of the Japanese for centuries, and these ceramic works were regarded as treasure, especially on the part of the higher strata of society. Even after the Hideyoshi invasion of Korea in the sixteenth century, a little more than one hundred years later in 1719, with Japan under the rule of the Tokugawa Shogunate, on the occasion of Yoshimune's inauguration, Joseon (Yi Dynasty Korea) sent a large mission composed of some four hundred officials and auxiliary members, well cultured and literary, to Edo, today's Tokyo.

The Korean Mission (*Joseon Tsushinshi* in Japanese) departed Seoul in April, traveled to Busan, then on a fleet of ships proceeded to Tsushima, Kyushu, Osaka, Kyoto, Otsu,

1. Editor's Note: While the Ural-Altaic Hypothesis was pursued and accepted around its initial development, most linguistic scholars have questioned it, and it has been largely discredited.

Biwako Shizuoka, and Fuji Mountain, finally reaching Edo in September 1719. The Mission returned to Seoul in January 1720, taking nine months, and the journey was meticulously chronicled in a volume entitled *Kaiyuroku,* published in Japan.

I saw the remains of the Mission in numerous places in Japan, viewed a prominent [re]construction of the Mission "*Joseon Do* (Korea Road)" and learned of episodes where the Japanese were seeking access for elegant literary and artistic visitors to calligraphic writings or signatures. Even today, the folk drama "*Joseon Tsushinshi*" is performed in Japan, in Akita City, which is far north of Tokyo, out of range of the Mission's journey, in the *Warabi-za* (theater). Here it performs as part of the theater's regular repertoire: a rendition of "Korean Mission".

Years ago, I read an impressive book entitled *Kokyo Bojitaku* (*How can the Homeland be Forgotten?*) by Shiba Ryotaro, probably Japan's leading historical writer with the most prominent reputation. I learned many fascinating factual stories about the kidnapped Korean ceramic artisans. The kidnapped families were put on a Japanese ship, but most of the Japanese naval fleet was in harm's way, because in the Korean Channel, Admiral Lee Soonshin, with his able leadership and ingenuity constructing the *Turtle Boat,* managed to maintain Korea's naval superiority by sinking or damaging a large number of the Japanese ships.

Consequently, the ship carrying the kidnapped artisans was apparently severely damaged, drifting on the sea for days and ended up coasting to the shore of Kagoshima, the domain of Daimyo Shimazu Yoshihiro. Yoshihiro was of course pleasantly surprised and immediately accommodated the artisans, bestowing on them the samurai class title. Sometime later, I watched a fascinating NHK documentary about the battle of Namwon and the story of the descendants of the Korean ceramic artisans in Kagoshima, Japan. A Japanese General, Sayaka, commanded about two thousand troops who sided with the Joseon Kingdom, whereby the King awarded the surname Kim (Wulok) and the name, Chung Seon to those descendants residing north of Daegu, Korea.

As mentioned earlier, Namwon was the original home of Shim Soo Kwan, (Jin Jukan), currently a member of the thirteenth generation of the famous Satsuma Yaki ceramicist family of Kagoshima, who had been named the winner of the first prize at the Paris International Exhibition at the turn of the nineteenth century. Jin Jukan, a member of the twelfth generation of this family, with whom I had personal communications, passed away a few years ago. He appeared in the NHK documentary, and on his way to Chungsong where his Shim (Chungsong) ancestors were buried, he paid a visit to the home of the direct descendent of the Japanese General Sayaka. The fascinating irony is that this Japanese descendent, in a traditional Korean dress and headgear, was reading his ancestor's message to the following generations in the Korean language, while Jin Jukan, in a normal business outfit, coat and tie, was trying to understand the message (spoken in Korean) through an interpreter. As a Japanese descendent who could not speak Japanese in the traditional Korean mourning garment, this descendant bowed and paid respect in front of the tombs of his original ancestors up on the hill surrounded by pine trees *chungsong* (green pine).

Shiba Ryotaro (his surname is that of the Grand Chinese Historian of the Han Dynasty and this name in kanji means the "respectful first son from far away") starts his book with a puzzling observation on the billboard at the entrance to Kagoshima City which says: "Don't fall behind Togo-senpai!" To him, along with almost all Japanese, the surname Togo is identified with the historically famous admiral who defeated the Russian Fleet during the Russo-Japanese War in the Korean Channel (Genkai Tana), Tōgō Heihachirō. Shiba discovered some fascinating facts about the descendants of the Koreans who landed on the Kagoshima coast.

Among the forty-seven kidnapped families from Namwon was one family with the surname Park, and one of the descendants of the Park family was Tōgō Shigenori, the Foreign Minister of Japan who declared war with the United States in 1941, and returned in 1945 to accept its unconditional surrender.

In 1922, despite the strenuous objections of Tōgō's family, he married a German woman, the widow of noted architect George de Lalande, who has designed numerous buildings in Japan and its empire, including the Japanese General Government Building in Seoul, which served as the capitol building for Presidents Syngman Rhee, Chang Myon, and Park Chung Hee's governments. Regrettably, it was demolished by the Kim Yongsam Regime. As a loyal and able diplomat, Tōgō was living up to the expectations of his adopted country in *datsuaron* "getting away from Asia" to acquire western knowledge, even choosing a German wife.

Tōgō was adamantly against war with the United States and the other western powers. In October 1941, he became Foreign Minister and it was his signature on the declaration of war with the United States, as he disliked pressing the responsibility of the failure of diplomacy on others. As part of a more reconciliatory policy towards the western powers, he announced on January 21, 1942, that the Japanese government would uphold the Geneva Convention, even though Japan did not sign it. On September 1, 1942, he resigned his post as Foreign Minister.

At the War Tribunal, Tojo Hideki, the Wartime Prime Minister, was sentenced to death by hanging in 1945, and it is interesting to note that before his arrest by the U.S. Military Police, Tojo tried to commit suicide with his own pistol, having marked his heart with colored ink. He missed the shot and failed. His cowardly act was a vivid contrast to the act of Seppuku, *harakiri* without a *Kaushaku* "terminal second" by General Anami Korechika, Minister of the Army, who suffered more than twenty hours of tortuous pain to end his life.

Anami's courageous act came after using his words "Over my dead body, *washino no shikabe o koete!*" to block the young insurgent officers leading a coup to take over the Imperial Palace after Emperor Hirohito's unconditional surrender statement. Anami intended to continue to fight the War to the last man. In another example, General Yamashita Tomoyuki, who was demoted by Tojo after the brilliant victory in Malaysia to secure Manchuria, was assigned to fight in the Philippines toward the end of the war and in defeat Yamashita courageously faced his own execution, as ordered by the War Tribunal.

Tōgō, on the other hand, was sentenced to 20 years imprisonment and died with chronic disease in Sugamo Prison in 1950. On one occasion, his daughter Togo Ise, *hapa* in Hawaiʻi with her German mother, came to Honolulu, and we had a wonderful dinner and a very pleasant and informative conversation.

I also learned from my professional friend, Professor Honjo of Tokyo University, Director of the United Nations Regional Planning Center in Nagoya, that his younger brother was Togo's adopted son-in-law. Small world. Togo's grandson served as Ambassador to Russia and retired. My friends who served in the Ministry of Foreign Affairs told me that Togo's nickname within the Ministry was Mr. Park.

For both sides, Korea and Japan, the ancestors' message to their descendants was to do better than those of neighbors in the host countries. An interesting fact about the descendants of Japan's General Sayaka, endowed with the surname Kim, is that a prominent Government leader, Kim Chi Yeol, who served as Minister of Justice and subsequently as Minister of Home Affairs during the Park Chung Hee government, was referred to pleasantly as "Japan Kim." This is a poetic irony, as a Korean descendent was heading the Ministry of Foreign Affairs in Japan and the Japanese were leading the Korean Ministry of Home Affairs.

In the mid-nineteenth century, Japan, faced with constant encroachment by the West, went through major upheavals in the course of its transformation from isolation to the opening of the country to the West.

The subsequent and rapid modernization of Japan during the Meiji Restoration and its turn toward the West made Japan a strong nation economically and militarily, understood as *Fukoku Kyohei* (rich nation/strong military) and in many ways was a model subsequently for lagging nations such as China and Korea.

In any historical process there are both negative and positive aspects. Until the late nineteenth century, Korea was known as the Hermit Kingdom and viewed China as the center of the world, continuing to turn inward, maintaining its overly Sinified political system and upholding the traditional tributary system with Beijing at its center, while the globalizing world passed it by.

In the meantime, in Japan, about a half century earlier in 1868, the Meiji revolution had swept away the Tokugawa *Bakufu* (military regime), which had espoused isolation for more than two centuries, launching a new era by opening to the world and to development, bringing in Western technology and ideas with the Japanese spirit (*Wakon Seisai*). This process of modernization touched upon almost every aspect of Japanese society, from clothing to the constitution, from the legal system to the educational system. The Japanese followed the so-called policy of *datsuaron* (getting away from Asia and gaining access to Western know-how), a logic espoused by Fukuzawa Yukichi, founder of Keio University. Yukichi's photo appears on the Japanese 10,000 yen banknote.

The Japanese regarded China and Korea as technologically backward. By blending East Asian values together with Western technology and science, Japan was able to expedite the process of modernization and economic development. By the turn of the century, one generation after the Meiji revolution, Japan had become the only modern power in Asia that was able to challenge the Western powers.

Geographically, the provinces on Japan's Sea coast, Niigata, Toyama, and Tottori, for example, were the principal gates to the continent and the center of civilization. China and the Korean Peninsula evolved in the backyard of Japan. *Ura Nihon* is a disparaging term and the Pacific coast developed into Japan's major corridor to the West and the Pacific.

Korea's long history of seclusion ended partly as a result of the Japanese policy of colonial expansion, which forcibly opened it to trade under the 1876 Korean-Japanese Treaty of Commerce.

The historic drama surrounding the ending of the Yi Dynasty at the turn of the nineteenth century and the subsequent annexation of Korea by Japan in 1910 was a national disaster and a tragedy.

Through my late father-in-law, Chun Taek Bu, who served as Permanent Secretary of the YMCA in Seoul and cooperated in a special education program for teaching handicapped children, the skills of "seven treasure" were introduced to Lady Lee Bang Ja (Li Fusako in Japanese), a member of the last lineage of the Yi Dynasty.

Lady Lee came from a small group of Japanese royal families linked directly to the Emperor's ancestral lineage. Aimed at a successful colonization of Korea, Japan, under the slogan of "Naisen Ittai" (integration of Korea and Japan as a whole) undertook intermarriages between the members of the royal families on both sides, as was the practice in the history of international relations. On the Korean side, after the dethroning of Emperor Sunjong, the crown prince Lee Eun, with the endowed title of *Yongchinwang*, was taken to Tokyo at a young age and schooled in elite military schools, from *Yonen Gakko* to the Military Academy, and promoted to Lieutenant General in 1941. During one of Lady Lee's occasional visits to Hawai'i in connection with her community social work, we invited her to our home on a hill at Halekoa Drive and we listened to fascinating stories of her life. She gave us a copy of her published memoir.

Lady Lee was shocked to read the nuptial announcement of her own engagement to Prince Lee in the newspaper. Her father, an Army General, had never mentioned a word about it. Lady Fusako was apparently one of the most eligible bridal candidates for Emperor Showa when he was the crown prince. We were impressed with her kind, modest, and graceful disposition. Her noble life was difficult, to say the least, despite all the pomp and circumstance inherent in a luxurious residence in the center of Tokyo. Her residence was later developed into one of Japan's most beautiful first-class hotels, Akasaka Prince Hotel.

Once, the former Governor of Hawai'i and East-West Center Board Chairman George Ariyoshi, and I, representing the East-West Center with representatives of our cooperating institutions in Japan, held a meeting at the Prince Hotel's only remaining structure—a sizable conference room that used to function as a reception room for Prince Lee. Most impressive and memorable was Lady Fusako's reflection that her happiest time was the one and a half years during which her husband and son lived together in a small apartment near MIT, where her son Lee Gu was studying architecture. She told us how much she enjoyed the freedom of shopping at grocery stores, cooking and enjoying meals together like ordinary people without the constraint of rituals and being monitored.

Mr. and Mrs. Ariyoshi at NEAEF meeting in Japan (2018)

At our home, we still have hanging on the wall her beautiful calligraphy "*All goes well with family harmony.*" At the end of the War, the Prince Lee family became stateless and at the same time all the noble perks, services, and provisions for essential goods such as food and other necessities were terminated. With no experience in handling monetary instruments and household affairs, they were in a dire situation, and to survive they had to buy rice along with other basic food supplies. To acquire the basic necessities and to pay for educational expenses for Gu, they used the land of their residence as collateral for the exchange and over the course of time frittered away a substantial portion of their assets.

That evening for dinner, we took Lady Lee to a Japanese teppanyaki restaurant and during the dinner, the Japanese chef serving us in front of the grill, having heard our conversation in Japanese, asked Lady Lee: "*Nihon no kata desu ka?* Are you Japanese?" I was wondering how she would respond, and was amazed at her gracious and thoughtful reply. "*Nihon de sunda koto arimasu,* I once lived in Japan." It was a difficult question for her, being a close relative of the Japanese Emperor. Her son, Lee Gu, after receiving his degree in architecture from MIT, worked for the renowned architect,

I. M. Pei, who designed the buildings for the East-West Center. As Pei's assistant, he left an architectural legacy in the form of a twelve-story structure: a graduate student dormitory called *Hale Mānoa*.

It was during the Park Chung Hee government in the 1960s, after the Syngman Rhee and subsequent regimes, that the family of Prince Lee was restored as Korean nationals. The government provided the courtesy, after the Prince passed away, for Lady Lee and her son Gu to return to Naksunje inside Changdeok Palace and assume Seoul as their residence.

Kant's Universal Law of Nature and the law of thermodynamics in the natural sciences predicate that any system can develop or grow to a higher level only in an open environment that allows the system to exchange energy, substance, and information with the outside world (Song Jian).

The opening of a country and interaction and exchange with the outside can in no way be denied as positive in terms of bringing about changes and progress in intellectual, scientific, economic, and social development. Would Korea have opened its door to the outside without being forced by Japan or another major power? That is a moot question. If left alone, it could have taken a long time, perhaps decades.

Dr. Song Jian visiting our home in Honolulu (circa mid-1980s)

Family photo taken in commemoration of receiving Mugunghwa Jang from Korea (circa early 1990s)

From my understanding, xenophobic tendencies and policies based on Confucian[2] ethics and traditions had prevailed for centuries in East Asia; in Japan for more than two centuries and in China for more than four and half. Given the strong resistance to change, anything short of a major revolution or the imposition of foreign domination would not have cracked the Hermit Kingdom open.

2. The term Confucian is used here to refer to the established ethical system of China, Korea, and Japan, which was derived from the synthesis of the traditional cultural values espoused by Confucius and his followers and subsequently influenced by elements of Taoism, Legalism, Mohism, and even Buddhism, and in the case of Korea and Japan, by Shamanism.

21

THE WORLD FERTILITY SURVEY

The World Fertility Survey (WFS) was one of the most important and largest international undertakings in demographic data collection and analysis of the twentieth century. Between 1973 and 1984, 66 countries carried out comparable surveys of human fertility. Forty-four of these were developing countries that received substantial financial and technical assistance channeled through WFS headquarters. Thus, an impressive geographical coverage was achieved, though some of the largest countries (China, India, Brazil, and the Soviet Union) declined to participate. Despite this, China was collaborating with EWPI.

The idea for this international program probably originated with Reimert Ravenholt, the forceful head of the Office of Population at the U.S. Agency for International Development (AID) and with whom I had a good working relationship. The program was intended as a means to resolve conflicting assessments of the fertility impact of family planning programs. The United Nations Fund for Population Activities (UNFPA) gave its support for the project and these two organizations became the dominant financial sponsors of the WFS, contributing about one half billion U.S. dollars combined.

Coordination of the enterprise was entrusted to the International Statistical Institute (ISI) based in the Netherlands, which brought the necessary scientific respectability and political independence. ISI was revitalized after WWII by my mentor, the late Stuart A. Rice, who served as permanent honorary chairman. The institute appointed the eminent British statistician Maurice Kendall (1907–1983) to head the program, which, at his insistence, was based in London. Thus, this unique program was funded by two US-based organizations, managed in the Netherlands, and executed in the United Kingdom.

Because of its mandate to yield internationally comparable data, the WFS developed core instruments to be used in all developing countries. These consisted of a household schedule or roster, and a more detailed questionnaire to be administered to ever-married women of reproductive age. Single women were also included in some surveys. Only three of the 44 surveys also canvassed husbands. The core questionnaire for women included complete marriage and pregnancy histories, and sections on socioeconomic background.

It was a great honor for me to be appointed as the most junior member of the WFS Committee to provide technical oversight of WFS activities and operations. I had to travel to London twice a year on a special redeye flight. The head of the technical staff of the World Fertility Survey at the time was Roderick Little, PhD, who made regular progress reports to the committee. Little came in a big way, to become the current Distinguished University Professor of Biostatistics and Director of Survey Research Center at the University of Michigan.

In London, the committee meetings took place at a hotel in a small conference room and the members sat closely without much "social distancing." I was usually surrounded by my former professor, Phil Hauser of Chicago, my former boss, Ron Freedman of Michigan, Ansley Coale of Princeton,

Bill Brass of the London School of Hygiene and Tropical Medicine—so-called giants of population studies. Sir Maurice Kendall, with a cigar in his right hand, would be chairing the meeting, sitting behind a white cloth-covered table. During a good part of the meeting, he closed his eyes as if dozing, and his right hand that held the lit cigar between his fingers would come down bit by bit, and all of us around the table watched curiously. Phil Hauser would wink at me as if to indicate the cigar would touch the table and burn the cloth. When the presentation and discussion were finished, Sir Maurice would wake up and with eyes wide open, make a succinct substantive summary of what took place, plus his conclusion for the session. Having seen Sir Maurice chairing the meeting like this every year, all of us got used to his idiosyncratic charm. We were not surprised to find that in his Who's Who entry, his hobby was noted as "Sleeping."

John Cleland, a former student of Bill Brass, served once as President of IUSSP (International Union for Scientific Study of Population) and co-published a volume in 1987, *The World Fertility Survey: An Assessment* (Oxford University Press, 1987). An interesting footnote on John Cleland is that years ago in the 1990s, in my capacity as chairman, I invited John to EWPI as a member of the high-profile evaluation team for the Nihon University Population Research Institute (NUPRI). John Cleland told me after the meeting that he had a trip planned to Iwate-ken in Northern Japan to see his relatives on his grandmother's side, which sounded odd coming from an Englishman. He said his trip to Japan would be unforgettable and had a very special meaning for him, and he revealed to me that on his grandmother's side, a great aunt had married Nitobe Inazo, the man depicted on the banknote of *5000 yen* in Japan. He was looking forward to meeting their descendants. This was the aftermath of an English-Japanese romance from more than a century ago. Nitobe (1862–1933), the author of *Bushido: The Soul of*

Japan, known as an educator and founder of Tokyo Women's University (promoting women's rights), was devoted to "bridging the Pacific Ocean to the West" and peace, contributing a great deal to the Westernization and modernization of Japan. That Nitobe discouraged monetary value for a higher goal, yet his photo was placed on the banknote, is a pleasant irony.

Part III

All chapters in part III, except chapter 22, are derived from the notes and records of the Hawai'i Asia-Pacific Institute/ Northeast Asia Economic Forum and were compiled posthumously.

22

A SIMPLIFIED EXPLANATION OF THE OWN-CHILDREN METHOD OF FERTILITY ESTIMATION

Robert Retherford

Lee-Jay Cho is very well known in the fields of demography and population studies for his pioneering work on the own-children method of fertility estimation. The fact that the method is used in so many countries around the world by census and statistical offices and academic researchers is testament not only to Lee-Jay's academic ability, but also to his organizational and political abilities. During the decades I worked with Lee-Jay on the own-children project I learned a great deal from him. We had a great working relationship, and we also had many good times together. I have many fond memories of Lee-Jay and miss him very much.

Given the important role that the own-children method played in Lee-Jay's life, I thought it would be appropriate and useful to provide a description of how the method works for readers who are not familiar with fertility estimation methods, and to discuss its significance. I have tried, with moderate success, to make this description easy to understand and short.

The own-children method of fertility estimation is typically applied to census data or household survey data.

The defining characteristic of censuses and household surveys is that entire households, rather than individuals, are the basic units of data collection. The census (or survey) identifies one person in the household as head of household and collects, for all other household members, information on relation to head of household—e.g., wife of head, son of head, sister of head, grandson of head, etc., including a "no relation" category. Also collected, for each household member, are age, sex, marital status, number of children ever born, and other individual characteristics of interest, such as educational attainment, that are included in the census. Also collected are a number of household characteristics, such as urban/rural residence.

The own-children method focuses on children in the household who are aged 0–14 in completed years of age. (Fifteenth birthday is the cutoff age; age 14 in completed years means anywhere from fourteenth birthday up to but not including fifteenth birthday.) Children aged 0–14 were born during the 15-year period preceding the census. A child aged 0 in completed years at the time of the census was born sometime during the first year before the census; a child aged 1 in completed years was born sometime during the second year before the census; and a child aged 14 in completed years was born sometime during the fifteenth year before the census. Children aged 15 or older are usually not considered in applications of the own-children method, because many of these children no longer live in the same household as their mothers and therefore cannot be matched to their mothers. Matching of children to mothers living in the same household is the core feature of the own-children method. Matched children are referred to in the method as "own children."

Children aged 0–14 are matched to mothers primarily by means of the relation-to-head question. For example, if a woman is wife of head, and a child is son of head, that woman is identified by the own-children computer program as the mother of that child. The matching procedure also checks for consistency with other information, such as whether the age difference between mother and child is within the acceptable range and whether the mother already has as many children matched to her as she says she has ever borne. Each matched child in the age range 0–14 can be classified by the child's own age and the child's mother's age.

In the own-children method, possible mothers (including women who are not ultimately matched to a child in the same household) are aged 15–64 at the time of the census. A woman aged 64 at the time of the census was 49 years of age at the start of the fifteenth year before the census. The own-children method considers age 15 to be the minimum age of mother at childbirth and 49 to be the maximum age of mother at childbirth. The age ranges 0–14 for children and 15–64 for women allow estimation of a complete set of age-specific fertility rates (ASFRs) by single years of age, spanning ages 15–49, for each of the 15 calendar years before the census.

The basic logic of the own-children method is most easily understood by considering a simple hypothetical example. Suppose a small census, taken on January 1, 2000, in which 302 children aged 0 at the time of the census are matched to mothers aged 24 at the time of the census, and suppose that the total number of women aged 24 at the time of the census is 1,050. The 302 children aged 0 were born during the first year before the census, i.e., during the year 1999, and the 1,050 women aged 24 on January 1, 2000, were aged 23 one year ago on January 1, 1999. One can compute a preliminary age-specific fertility rate for women aged 23, pertaining to calendar year 1999, as 302/1050 = 0.288 births per woman per year or, equivalently, 288 births per thousand women per year. Using other combinations of child's age and mother's age at the time of the census, one can compute a complete set of preliminary ASFRs by single years of age for each of the 15 calendar years preceding the census.

These ASFRs are preliminary for three main reasons: (1) They do not take into account that some children and some women died between the calendar year of interest and the time of the census. (2) They also do not take into account the earlier births corresponding to unmatched (non-own) children at the time of the census. And (3) they differ slightly from conventional ASFRs that are computed using birth registration data on number of births in the numerator of an ASFR and an intercensal estimate of mid-year numbers of women in the denominator of that ASFR. The own-children computer program includes procedures for taking care of all three of these deficiencies, so that, in the end, the own-children ASFRs that are printed out by the computer program are comparable to conventional ASFRs that utilize birth registration data on mother's age at childbirth.

In many developing countries, vital registration systems are underdeveloped and many births are not registered, so that conventional ASFRs are underestimated. But censuses in these same countries are often fairly accurate. It is in these countries that the own-children method of fertility estimation is especially useful.

In a typical application of the own-children method, all births are more or less accounted for. But the age pattern of the ASFRs can be thrown off a bit, as in the case of adopted children, whose adoptive mothers tend to be older than their biological mothers, resulting in downwardly biased ASFRs at younger reproductive ages and upwardly biased ASFRs at older reproductive ages. On the other hand, if one simply adds up the single-year-of-age ASFRs in a particular calendar year to get a total fertility rate (TFR) for that calendar year, these biases tend to cancel out. The TFR (total number of births per woman, as explained below) is what is typically reported in newspapers as "the birth rate." The TFR is the main fertility measure of interest to demographers, policymakers, family planning program managers, and journalists. It is an attractive measure, because "total births per woman" is a concept that is readily understood by everyone. There are, however, some fine points of interpretation of the TFR that are not immediately obvious but are important to understand.

How is it that we can interpret the sum of the ASFRs as the number of births that a woman will eventually have? To answer this question, it is useful to think of an ASFR as births per woman per year instead of births per thousand women per year. When we sum the ASFRs specified by single years of woman's age we do the following addition: births per woman per year at age 15 plus births per woman per year at age 16 plus births per woman per year at age 17 plus . . . plus births per woman per year at age 49. Expressing the sum of the ASFRs in this way makes clear that the TFR is the total number of births that a woman would have if, hypothetically, she lived through her reproductive years experiencing the ASFRs pertaining to the particular calendar year under consideration. This explains why it is that we can calculate a TFR for each single calendar year, right up to the beginning of the current calendar year.

It is worth noting that this calculation and interpretation of the TFR is similar in some respects to the calculation and interpretation of life expectancy. A person's life expectancy is typically defined as how long a person would live if, hypothetically, that person lived through his or her life experiencing the set of single-year age-specific mortality rates pertaining to a particular calendar year. Just as in the case of the TFR, that calendar year could be the most recently completed calendar year.

The own-children method can also provide estimates of ASFRs and TFRs by characteristics, as long as those characteristics do not change much as a woman moves simultaneously through age and calendar time. In reality, however, characteristics such as a woman's rural-urban residence and especially her number of years of education often do change over her reproductive age span. This means that 15-year trends in own-children estimates of the TFR by characteristics such as education are often difficult to interpret, given that the census

Dr. Robert Retherford

records years of education only at the time of the census, not at the time of each of a woman's childbirths. For this reason, own-children estimates of the TFR by characteristics such as education are often published only for calendar years close to the census and in some cases only for the year immediately preceding the census. Such estimates of the TFR by education are still very useful, however, because birth certificates do not contain information on mother's educational attainment, so that calculation of conventional ASFRs and TFRs by education is not possible, and because a mother's level of educational attainment typically has a strong effect on her fertility.

23

THE ESTABLISHMENT OF THE NORTHEAST ASIA ECONOMIC FORUM

Dramatic social and political changes in the late 1980s, culminating in the end of the Cold War, created new opportunities for broad and bold thinking about economic development of the long-neglected Northeast Asia region. There was recognition that in this positive political climate, Northeast Asia's complementary human, natural, and capital resources could be cooperatively mobilized to generate dynamic new economies throughout the region.

NEAEF was established in response to the new opportunities for broad and bold thinking about economic development that were created by the end of the Cold War. Dr. Cho was quick to recognize and promote the idea that in this more positive political climate, Northeast Asia's complementary human, natural, and capital resources could be cooperatively mobilized to generate dynamic new economies throughout the region.

The idea of a Northeast Asian Economic sphere first began to gain momentum with the 1988 Niigata Conference on the Sea of Japan, organized by former Japanese Minister of Foreign Affairs Dr. Okita Saburo and Dr. Lee-Jay Cho of the East-West Center. Around the same time, Dr. Song Jian, Director of the State Science and Technology Commission of the People's Republic of China, was considering the possibilities of developing the Tumen River Basin.

In 1991, Dr. Cho established the Northeast Asia Economic Forum (NEAEF), a regional nongovernmental organization to sponsor and facilitate research, networking, and dialogue related to the economic cooperation and development of Northeast Asia.

The establishment of NEAEF and its work in bringing former adversaries in Northeast Asia together for joint research and cooperation was a result of Dr. Cho's many years cultivating relations and trust among government officials and academics throughout the Northeast Asia region and the United States. NEAEF has held meetings and conducted joint research projects in China, Japan, Mongolia, Russia, the United States, South Korea, and North Korea.

NEAEF is the only nongovernmental regional organization in which the six nations of Northeast Asia and the United States have been consistent and active participants. Forum membership was extended to interested individuals and institutions both within the region and internationally. The Forum's secretariat is located in Honolulu, Hawai'i.

Dr. Cho's other achievements in promoting peace and cooperation in the Asia-Pacific region include parliamentarian education activities on population, development, and the environment, for example, the 1992 Asia-Pacific Parliamentarian Leaders Forum in Hawai'i, which brought parliamentarian leaders together to jointly address population and environment concerns.

In cooperation with partners from China, Japan, and South Korea, Dr. Cho, through NEAEF, organized and sponsored annual expert working group meetings for 17 years on energy and the environment which have taken place in Japan, China, Korea, Russia, Europe, and the United States (Alaska and Hawai'i).

24

THE PAN-PACIFIC COMMUNITY AND PECC

The Stepping-Stone to APEC

In 1980, during the Ohira Masayoshi regime, Foreign Minister Okita Saburo initiated the proposal of a Pacific Basin Community, which later evolved into the Pacific Economic Cooperation Council (PEC). Prime Minister Ohira and Dr. Okita Saburo went to Australia to initiate the pacific community idea jointly with Australian Prime Minister Malcom Fraser. Dr. Cho had been professionally acquainted with Dr. Okita Saburo and had served on the same committees for international economic and demographic issues.

The Pacific Basin Community proposal included as initial members: the market economy countries Japan, USA, Australia, New Zealand, Canada, and five ASEAN countries grouped as one member. South Korea was not included because of the North and South Korea division.

Dr. Cho was serving as President Pro Tem of the East-West Center then and was called by the Deputy Assistant Secretary of the U.S. State Department to help out in solving the proposed member issues, given his close professional and personal relationships with Dr. Okita Saburo in Japan and Dr. Widjoyo Nitisastro, Chairman of Indonesian Ministry of

National Development Planning (BAPPENAS) and Coordinating Minister for Economic Ministries for Indonesia and others in Southeast Asia.

Dr. Cho flew to Jakarta, Indonesia, and had a long meeting with Minister Widjoyo who was positive on regional economic cooperation but would not risk going into the big Pacific framework immediately. Dr. Cho returned to Tokyo and conveyed a long-term positive view of a Pacific economic community on the part of Indonesia. It was a significant contribution in the initial and formative stages of PECC and ultimately, APEC.

25

THE ESTABLISHMENT OF DIPLOMATIC RELATIONS BETWEEN THE PEOPLE'S REPUBLIC OF CHINA AND THE REPUBLIC OF KOREA

In the 1960s and 1970s, humankind was faced with challenges in dealing with the global issue of population explosion, and an increasing number of nations joined the massive international effort to cope with an explosive growth of population, and China was no exception. The pressing issue of population explosion brought about the serendipitous encounter of a Chinese scientist in Beijing and a Korean demographer in Hawai'i.

Convening at the East-West Center, Drs. Song Jian and Lee-Jay Cho communicated with each other on the common topic of population across the national border of the two countries without diplomatic relations. They became lifelong friends.

The two met in Beijing, and Song and his junior colleague Dr. Yulingyuan were invited to the East-West Population Institute for cooperative research on Chinese population. Because Song was promoted to the Vice Minister of Aerospace, only Yu was able to come to Hawai'i to undertake productive and innovative research of major subsequent impact on China's population policy.

Song made significant scientific contributions to demographic science through his seminal research and publication of technical monographs in the United States. In 1985, Song Jian was promoted to Director of China's State Science and Technology Commission (SSTC), which had always been headed by a deputy premier and which oversees several ministries and related agencies, such as environment and ocean affairs.

Cooperation with the East-West Center and SSTC expanded beyond population issues into other functional areas' cooperation in water resources, management of electric power generation, and coastal development issues, which led to the idea of Tumen River area development. The collaboration with SSTC triggered the close cooperation with the Planned Births Commission and the State Statistics Office and led to the regional economic cooperation issues with State Council Development Research Center headed by Dr. Ma Hong who, under the leadership of Deng Xiaoping, developed the basic strategy for opening China's economy with former Prime Minister Zhu Rongji as one of his assistants.

Dr. Cho was informed that in the beginning the subject of South Korea was basically taboo and there was strong opposition to developing any relationship with South Korea due firstly to the strong bond and ties backed up by a formidable close network in China developed by North Korea and secondly, stereotype perception of South Korea as "a ruthless military dictatorship."

In 1983, Song Jian arranged for Lee-Jay Cho to present a lecture to high government officials on the subject of the Economic Development of Korea under the leadership of President Park Chung Hee. His presentation was well received, especially the specific features of development policies that would be helpful in the future economic development of China. Song Jian, as a scientist in a leadership position, was most effective in correcting the distortions with facts and providing an objective view of South Korea. Equipped with truths and facts, he took the enormous risk of engaging in the preparatory work required for developing a diplomatic relationship between the two countries, and in his interview with *Joseon Monthly* he stated that Dr. Lee-Jay Cho was then more at risk.

Subsequently, China's Foreign Minister Qian Qichen led a delegation to North Korea for a meeting with Leader Kim Il Sung to inform him of China's decision to establish a formal diplomatic relationship with South Korea. When the shocking message was conveyed, there was an uneasy silence of disbelief. Foreign Minister Qichen hastily returned to Beijing. In early 1991, South Korea and China exchanged trade offices and in mid-1992 the Republic of Korea and the PRC established a formal diplomatic relationship. (This is based on the record of Zhang Tingyuan, First Ambassador to ROK.)

At the 14th Northeast Asia Economic Conference in Shenyang China in 2005, President Roh Tae Woo stated: "I want to acknowledge the historical roles played by Dr. Song Jian, former Vice-Premier of China, and by Dr. Lee-Jay Cho, the founding chairman of NEAEF, in the history of the formal (diplomatic) relationship between the two countries."

26

THE TUMEN RIVER BASIN AND OTHER PROJECTS

An extraordinary cooperative development initiative, the Tumen River project, now sadly inactive in a region again threatened by war, was envisioned by NEAEF as the establishment of joint special zones containing geographically proximate areas of China, North Korea, and the Soviet Union. It was a significant economic development initiative during Lee-Jay Cho's tenure, intended to reduce the probability of conflict in the region, by processing resources in identified zones and exporting them via the Tumen River to markets in Japan, Korea, and other Pacific countries. Moreover, the proposed development involved the Yanbian region in China, where a substantial population of ethnic Koreans reside. Thus, it was ambitiously envisioned to also provide opportunities for indirect cooperation between the two Koreas, North and South.

According to notes from related NEAEF meetings, in North Korea's view, the Tumen River project was viewed as the initial experiment of a joint venture with South Korea as its first and foremost investor: a first step toward the reunification of the Korean peninsula. China's interest was to restore the trade and cultural linkages through the region with the ultimate goal of building a "land bridge" between northeast

China and the Japan Sea. Japan's motivation, not strictly economic, was to contribute to overall world development. Russia expressed its preference for the idea of designing a large development zone from Vladivostok to Chongiin as proposed by China. The rationale for the zone would be to encourage foreign capital and accelerate development by increasing the supply of goods and services available and increasing exports.

The overall Tumen River Project was a visionary initiative, conceived to normalize political relations between Japan, Russia, and North Korea. South Korea and Japan would achieve easier access to cheap labor and natural resources in short supply in their countries. Japan and South Korea would be able to diversify their export market. Further, the development of the Tumen River mouth would pave the way for North Korean and Russian ports to engage in trade with other Northeast Asian countries.

Parliamentary Seminars

In the decades of the 1980s and early 1990s, Dr. Cho organized and conducted a series of Parliamentarian seminars throughout the Asia-Pacific region. The Asia Pacific Parliamentarian Leaders Forum (APPLY) 1992, organized jointly by the Hawai'i-Asia Pacific Institute (an umbrella organization for NEAEF) and the National Assembly of the Republic of Korea, Office of the Speaker (Park Jun Kyu) was convened in Kona, Hawai'i in 1992 under the umbrella theme of "The Future of the Asia-Pacific" to discuss the issues of environment, population, the current situation in Russia, and more.

Northeast Asian Bank for Cooperation and Development (NEABCD)

Dr. Cho's leadership for establishing a Northeast Asian Bank for Cooperation and Development (NEABCD) was envisioned as a mechanism to attract capital for regional development projects, to further the economic cooperation and regional integration of Northeast Asian nations, and to promote social and economic development within Northeast Asia, in a fiscally, socially, and environmentally responsible manner.[1]

Energy and Environment

In cooperation with Japan's Committee for the Promotion of East Asia Energy Community, Dr. Cho and Dr. Taro Nakayama, Member of Parliament and Chairman of the Commission for Promotion of Asia Energy Community (CPAEC) jointly organized and sponsored a series of annual NEAEF expert meetings with support from the Ministry of Foreign Affairs of Japan and other institutions in Northeast Asian countries.

The Annual Meeting Series on Energy Cooperation in Northeast Asia began in October 1999 as a major theme for regional cooperation. The initial meeting was held in conjunction with the Ninth Northeast Asia Economic Forum held in Tianjin, China, and was attended by prominent experts and policy makers such as Dr. Taro Nakayama, Former Foreign Minister of Japan; Mohammad Farhandi, who was then with the World Bank; and others from China, Japan, Korea, Mongolia, Russia, and the USA.

The first Honolulu Expert's Meeting on Natural Gas in Asia was held in Hawai'i in July 2000, and was the first

1. NEAEF held six meetings of the Ad-Hoc Committee for Establishing the Northeast Asian Bank for Cooperation and Development, the first of which was held in 1999. NEAEF also established the NEABCD Advisory and Steering Committee, chaired by Dr. Stanley Katz, former vice president of the Asian Development Bank. This complex initiative was not without difficulty, given the scope of its vision for regional cooperation and collaboration, and despite diligent efforts, this original vision was not achieved during Dr. Cho's lifetime.

in a series of working group meetings on energy and environment organized by the Northeast Asia Economic Forum (NEAEF) in collaboration with CPAEC with support from the Ministry of Foreign Affairs of Japan. The cooperating institutions included Japan Bank for International Cooperation (BIC), Japan National Oil Corporation (NOC), and Korea Gas Corporation.

As a result of these early conversations, Hawai'i has been discussed and is being examined as a major center and mode for clean energy through international cooperation, especially in collaboration with the Northeast Asian countries of Japan, China, and Korea.

27

PUBLICATIONS

In addition to his world-renowned work as a population demographer, Dr. Cho made many important academic contributions to studies of peaceful economic development. His investigations emphasized cross-cultural and comparative institutional perspectives. He authored and edited numerous publications in the field of population demography and economic development.

He initiated the Tiger Book Series (which continues today on the economic development of South Korea from a comparative and regional perspective). From 1991 to 2011, 17 books in the series were published under Dr. Cho's authorship. The first book in the series, *Economic Development in the Republic of Korea* (1991) was described by P. W. Kuznets as the "definitive work on such policies," meriting attention from anyone interested in the policy aspect of Korea's economic development." These books led to more policy-relevant research on the topic and influenced the work of the World Bank and its publication of the East Asia Miracles series.

Dr. Cho also developed the Project on Comparative Study of History Textbooks of Intermediate Schools in Northeast Asian Countries resulting in the publication in 2009/2010 in Korean, Chinese, and English of *Toward Regional Harmony and Community: A Comparative Study of History Textbooks and Cultural and Economic Exchange.*

Reflecting his deep and personal commitment to peace through mutual understanding, Lee-Jay was a keen student of linguistics and was fluent in English, Chinese, Japanese, and Korean. He was also an avid student of Chinese classical literature.

28

THE YOUNG LEADERS PROGRAM

In 2006, with a view to encouraging peace and cooperation among future generations, Dr. Cho launched the NEAEF Young Leaders Program (YLP), which was the precursor to the current Emerging Leaders Program (ELP). The YLP is a unique program to bring young leaders in academia, government, and business together in a different country of Northeast Asia and the United States every year for research and training in regional cooperation.

It encourages the consideration of a wide range of perspectives on regional economic, political, and social concerns, and examines interdisciplinary and cooperative approaches to problem-solving. Based on his vast experience and understanding of relations in the region, Dr. Cho aimed to encourage recognition among young leaders of the importance of lowering national barriers and creating networks of trust, good will, and effective communication.

The first year of the program was held in Khabarovsk, Russia and included 30 participants selected through a competitive application process from the US, Japan, China, Mongolia, South Korea, and Russia. Near and dear to Dr. Cho's heart, it is aimed at promoting cooperative study and research on Northeast Asia, encouraging the consideration of a wide range of perspectives on regional economic, political, and social concerns, and examining interdisciplinary and cooperative approaches to problem-solving.

From 2006 to 2019, the YLP was successfully implemented with support from the Freeman Foundation and other cooperating institutions in the US and Northeast Asian countries. The high quality and relevance of the program and participants have been sustained as attested by annual post program evaluations. The global pandemic interrupted the annual YLP program; however, the ELP has continued to carry on the YLP legacy, beginning with the first ELP cohort in 2022.

Dr. Lee-Jay Cho's decades of expertise in the areas of demography, economic development, and community and family studies were mirrored by his keen interest in inspiring future leaders to seek peace and cooperation in Northeast Asia. His legacy, embodied in the YLP, is to cultivate objectivity from a cross-cultural and comparative perspective; something he understood as valuable from an early age, which is more necessary than ever in building mutual understandings and friendly relations between countries.

It was his wish that his memoir be dedicated to tomorrow's future leaders.

Part IV

29

REFLECTIONS ON LEE-JAY CHO'S CONTRIBUTIONS TO POPULATION RESEARCH AND POLICY

Andrew Mason

It is a great honor to talk about Dr. Lee-Jay Cho and his contributions to population research and policy. I first met Lee-Jay in 1975 when I joined the Population Institute at the East-West Center and the Economics Department at the University of Hawai'i. The Population Institute was a young and dynamic institution. There were around two dozen researchers who had been recruited from the top research centers in the world—Berkeley, Chicago, and Michigan to name a few. We had a large staff of computer programmers, editors, graphic artists, program officers, fiscal staff, and others. At its peak, more than 50 people worked at the Population Institute and Lee-Jay Cho was the Director, the leader of this enterprise.

The Population Institute had a broad agenda with research on migration, health and mortality, fertility, population growth and its consequences. A major driver for population research in the early 1970s was rapid population growth—its causes and its consequences. Many of the Institute's activities, research, training, and collaboration, responded to THE population issue of the time.

One of Lee-Jay's most important contributions was improving the quality of demographic data, particularly data on the number of births. In many countries, systems for registering births were very incomplete. Thus, direct measurement of the number of births could not be relied on. However, census counts of the number of children could be used to estimate the number of births that preceded the census. Lee-Jay's research on the own-children method led to much better data about trends in fertility and about how those varied among socioeconomic groups. These methods have been refined and continue to be used today—much to Lee-Jay's credit.

The own-children method and other tools developed at the East-West Center had a much greater impact than most research because Lee-Jay and the Institute created tools and conducted training programs that helped to improve the quality of data throughout the Asia-Pacific region. More generally, programs at the Population Institute were successful because of Lee-Jay's commitment to quality and because of his integrity.

Lee-Jay succeeded in attracting the very best scholars and practitioners in Asia and the West to participate in our programs. He had an amazing ability to attract the top people to present their work and to collaborate with others. Why do I mention his integrity? Because of his leadership, the Population Institute built an enormous and valuable collection of data. In many cases, these data were not available elsewhere and could only be accessed under very strict conditions. A key ingredient of this approach is that the producers of important data were heavily involved in the use of that data. Very important research occurred at the Population Institute because of the trust that Lee-Jay built over many years.

Lee-Jay's most remarkable accomplishment during those years was his influence on policy. Much of this was carried on in the field rather than in Honolulu. He organized and led many activities and often these had a direct influence

Dr. Andrew Mason

on the ways in which countries conducted population policy. He always practiced QUIET diplomacy. I never knew him to lecture any decision-maker about the right way to do things. His approach was to give those who were succeeding an opportunity to share with those who might benefit from the successes of others. Lee-Jay practiced this quiet diplomacy at the highest levels of leadership around the Asia-Pacific region. Traveling with Lee-Jay on many occasions was quite the education for me, and I was constantly astonished to see the master at work.

30

A LETTER TO MY FATHER ON HIS 80TH BIRTHDAY

Ray Cho

Dear Dad,

Every so often, I find myself shaking my head and chuckling in disbelief. How did I end up being interested in sociology and economics? Why do I enjoy jogging? Why does it feel good to start my day with back exercises? When I look in the mirror, I'm starting to see someone maturing in a way I never imagined. As a kid, I always thought I would one day become my own unique person, and in many ways, I certainly have. But like many American kids, we don't want to completely accept the similarities we share with our parents, especially as the first generation born of immigrants. We want our own unique identity. Yet beneath a trivial sense of denial, I feel tremendously blessed. My dad passed along a few virtues that I will forever cherish.

First, I'm thankful for having a global and multicultural perspective. My dad introduced me to Japan, Korea, San Francisco, Chicago, Wisconsin, and more, not to mention Hawai'i. I was given a very special lens with which to view the world. Looking back, it's amazing the opportunities I was afforded. While some can claim to have a father who encourages world travel, few can claim to have a father who is a certified expert in world cultures. Back then, I wasn't always so enthusiastic. It wasn't my preference. It felt boring. It felt different. I didn't always like it because I wanted to do what other kids did. I thought they were the lucky ones. Many years later, I realized I was the lucky one all along.

The exposure by itself is a blessing, but it's also remarkable that I was encouraged to travel alone. Sure, it was lonely at times, but unbeknownst to me, I was learning self-sufficiency and independence. Also, the seeds of my intellectual curiosity were starting to bud. Little by little, through these journeys, I saw the possibility of what I could achieve on my own. I became unafraid to venture out and explore. Most others never left home. They rarely went out of their comfort zone. But to me, I find comfort in not staying in one place. I sometimes wished my father had spent more time with me growing up. But in another sense, I'm so grateful for the autonomy. It makes me think of my father's own journey to success, far away from his family. And like him, today, my survival instincts and global adaptability are well-tuned.

I also have to admit I hated jogging as a kid. I mean, really, really hated it. I cried, complained, and did whatever I could to avoid it. It was no fun. Today, I can routinely run five kilometers at a healthy pace without complaint. Most people I know can't even maintain a jogging pace even for a few minutes. Fresh air mixed with some self-discipline is not just beneficial to my health and morale; it also helps me in other aspects. It's improved my persistence and focus, which, when I look at the world around me, the lack of these qualities seems more unique than it should. I did not like being dragged out of the house, but now, I feel unaccomplished if I don't get my butt off the couch. Achievement requires some perspiration and even a little pain. It's hard to see that as a kid, but I clearly see it today.

Kids gravitate toward being lazy, and I'm certainly no exception. And while it felt like my father was taking my freedom away, the freedom I feel today has its roots in those same tough experiences. Thank you, Dad. It's you who helped sculpt my wings. They feel strong, and when I gaze at the horizon, I see possibility, and I feel confident. So, to the man who gave me the tools, while another decade has passed and a few more wrinkles may appear, what remains both vibrant and abundant is your passion. Whether traveling, working, or eating a steak, it's this unrelenting spirit that I am so grateful to have inherited. Happy Birthday, Dad. Please enjoy the day and remember that your legacy of diligence and worldly pursuits lives with me. You are the wind at my back, giving me that extra advantage, valuable when carrying the routine hazards of life.

With love,
Ray

31

A NOTE ABOUT MY FATHER

Jeremy Cho

Dear Reader,

First of all, I need to commend you for taking on this journey of learning about my father's fascinating life. Getting a true understanding of what my father did and how he saw the world is a tough nut to crack. It is a cultural and intellectual roller coaster—imagine how difficult it was for me as a child to explain what my father did to others. In short, I like to say that my father was an intercultural and intellectual consensus-builder. There is a general tendency to draw lines between cultures, nations, demographics, etc., but my father loved to find the universalities, the commonalities, the mutual benefits. He invited people to think in new ways, see things differently. It is an extreme curiosity that he ended up this way as he grew up in the midst of horrible conflict. He was an ethnic "zainichi" Korean living in Japan during a time when Japan occupied Korea. During WWII, he was attacked by U.S. airplanes. Just a few years later, he moved to Korea and entered conflict again directly—this time as an aid helping the U.S. military. Despite being immersed in the extreme violence of war and the heartbreaking personal losses associated with it, my father remained a gentle soul who was a deep and creative thinker.

He was the kind of person who would stop and look at the moon and wanted to let you know how beautiful it was—and there were so many levels to this. As a child, I recall him getting nostalgic when looking at the moon and, separately, singing along to funny-sounding Chinese poem songs on his Walkman while jogging. These things only connected later in my adult life as I was studying Chinese when he taught me the famous Tang-dynasty poem by Li Bai, Quiet Night Thought (静夜思), which opens with a scene of the moon and ends with a feeling of nostalgia. He'd tell you to shush and appreciate the moment if you barged in during a critically important part of a piece of great cinema or classical music performance. My own eclectic tastes are perhaps shaped by a combination of Disney and Akira Kurosawa, MTV and Vienna Philharmonic. And through these experiences in the arts, he'd always be able to connect to ideas in academics. He said he'd always liked to watch movies before a big exam and it was his realization that a movie was in fact a moving picture—snapshots in time—that inspired him to develop the Own-Children method of reconstructing fertility data from incomplete datasets for his PhD thesis. Decades later, this method is still being used to provide invaluable fertility statistics throughout the developing world.

He showed me, from a young age, that it wasn't necessarily about just the knowledge that you gain, but perhaps more importantly about the many ways that you could think. One of the most profound childhood moments of learning for me was when I was in the third grade, playing with a calculator at home. In school, I gained knowledge of the times table. But at home, my father imparted a new way of thinking. My father told me that every year, for every 1000 people in the world, 10 people die. He walked through the calculations with me to figure out how many people die in the world every second.

At the time, when the world population was around 6 billion, I found that two people died every second. This was supremely shocking to me, especially as someone who hadn't really dealt with death too much at that point in life. This disturbing fact had made the world so big and gloomy; it was a difficult and painful idea to grasp. But I also went through every calculation step, punching in all the numbers and operations into the calculator—I knew it had to be true. There wasn't a wrong step in the calculation. Everything made logical sense. But it was then that my father told me that for every 1000 people, 20 people are born every year. So that means that for every two people who pass, four babies are born! For every sorrow, there was double the joy—this reassured me and balanced my emotions. The world made sense again to my third-grade head. And more importantly, I stayed curious and fascinated. Even if I couldn't quite share that joy with some of my school classmates, it didn't matter; I knew that thinking this way was so addicting and empowering. You might say that this moment with my father had some impact in my life and my eventual career in academia, where I indulge myself in theory-heavy research, challenging problem solving, and teaching the most difficult but rewarding concepts.

Helping people see and think differently was what my father loved to do, and I hope this is apparent in this memoir. It came from his own experiences of stretching his mind. He welcomed people from conflicting geopolitical sides and encouraged dialogue through logic, promoting everyone to stretch their minds a bit. He knew that the world was smaller and friendlier when people gathered together in a room. People like to brush off world peace as a naive and fanciful idea. But for my father, the idea of peace, for some parts of his life, was literally a matter of life and death. It is perhaps very convenient to be pessimistic about the attainment of peace in a persistently challenging world of old and new conflict. But in my father's thoughts, it is perhaps essential to our survival and our duty to stretch our minds and undertake the challenges to achieve the optimistic outcome of peace. And I couldn't agree more, even with the world already quite different from when my father last saw it.

Jeremy

32

A YOUNG LEADER REMEMBERS

Stanley Chang

I woke up in a university hotel in Beijing, China, early one morning, still groggy. I'd gone to sleep late the night before working on a presentation about Mongolia's history, economy, and culture. All of us had been assigned to research and deliver a presentation on one of the countries represented in the Northeast Asia Economic Forum, but it could not be our own. Naturally, I'd chosen the country I knew the least about.

Over the buffet breakfast downstairs, I met with my fellow Team Mongolia members, who hailed from Korea, China, and Japan, to review our presentation, which we'd be delivering that afternoon. After making last-minute finishing touches, we joined the rest of the young leaders in the conference room that would be our home for the week. At 9am, we were all seated and ready for a presentation from a Japanese professor, Inoue Satoshi, on transportation and logistics in Northeast Asia. But our convenor, Dr. Lee-Jay Cho, was nowhere to be seen.

Just before someone was dispatched down the hall to watch for his entrance, the door burst open, and Dr. Cho was finally there. Gasps came from around the room. A thick, white gauze pad covered his left eye. Dried blood was visible on the tape and around his eye. Members of the group jumped out of their chairs, rushing to aid the octogenarian. Dr. Cho only laughed. "I fell in the shower last night and cut my forehead above my eye, but I'm OK now. Don't worry about me, sit down, and let's get started with Professor Inoue." And with that, the first session of the day began.

A friend of mine had contacted me about participating in the Northeast Asian Economic Forum (NEAEF) Young Leaders Program (YLP) toward the end of my City Council term in 2013 or 2014. He had just participated himself in the YLP in Vladivostok, Russia. I couldn't go because I was busy on the campaign trail for Congress. But after that campaign ended unsuccessfully, he reached out again, and I accepted.

That YLP summer in China was one of the defining moments of my life. I met lifelong friends that I still see today. In 2015, YLP was in Tianjin and Beijing. These were two of my favorite cities even before the trip, having spent time there growing up. Because I knew my way around a bit, I was able to organize weekend/free time excursions to places like the Wudadao (Five Avenues) in Tianjin and Yiheyuan (Summer Palace) in Beijing.

The best part of the program was meeting such great people from all over the world. We worked with each other in professional settings, like on presentations mentioned earlier, and in casual settings, for late night drinks on the weekend. That's how our relationships formed and deepened. On our first day, we were assigned to another person to introduce ourselves, and then introduce that person to the entire group. I introduced a half Chinese, half British student who'd attended both Eton College and Tsinghua University. We hit it off immediately and have seen each other many times over the years, including in Hong Kong and London.

I've also met with two of the other Chinese participants many times, in Hawai'i, Shanghai, and Hong Kong.

Many other participants eagerly joined our excursions, including those from Korea, Russia, and Japan. The excitement of making friends from such different backgrounds and countries didn't stop for the entire trip.

Our faculty and presenters were equally interesting. Dr. Cho, of course, was the guiding light. His unique background—an ethnic Korean born in Japan—who'd helped during the Korean War, and who'd personally experienced the racial rioting in Malaysia, who spoke excellent Korean, Japanese, English, and learned some Russian and even literary Chinese. His vision was a Northeast Asia connected so closely through links of trade and infrastructure that conflict would never happen again, and no one worked more passionately on bringing it to fruition. Showing up to participate fully in day after day of programming despite his head injury was just one example of his superhuman commitment.

One of my presentations was on the flashpoints between the countries, like Dokdo, which both Korea and Japan claim. I could tell Dr. Cho was a bit on edge during the whole presentation, but I managed to deliver it diplomatically enough that he didn't end it right there.

The other faculty members were also excellent, from Nankai University, Professor Liu, whose knowledge of Chinese politics and history was encyclopedic, to Professor Zhang, who spoke deliberately, but who provided some of the best translation from Chinese into English that I'd ever heard.

Not every presentation or field trip was strictly related to a serious topic like renewable energy policy. One afternoon, we visited the famous Beijing Film Academy, training ground for generations of Chinese movie stars, including Zhao Wei and Huang Xiaoming. We toured the displays of awards won by the graduates and the state-of-the-art recording studios, and our guides were current students. Their flawless complexions and sharp jawlines just may have been the most impressive things we saw on the entire program.

I realized later that Dr. Cho was as committed to these excursions on our own time as to the formal programming of the YLP. He knew that in international relations, as in anything else, relationships are everything. The backbone of relationship building was the opportunity to spend unstructured time together exploring a new city, sampling new cuisines, and drinking together. Occasionally he participated in a Young Leader-led activity, but he usually needed to spend his time working with his counterparts in that country.

I was invited to participate in another YLP in 2018, in Sendai, Japan, which was decorated with the colorful, flowing streamers of the Tanabata festival. This time, I was a presenter, not a Young Leader, and I'd only be able to stay a few days. I prepared a PowerPoint on the future of tourism, and this new cohort had a lot of questions about the Native Hawaiian community and culture. Even though I'd only be in town a few days, I took advantage of the opportunity to visit Matsushima Bay, one of Japan's top three most beautiful sightseeing spots; the Sendai Museum, with its many artifacts of the samurai lord Date Masamune; and even the Nikka Miyagikyo Whisky Distillery, where I gained a new appreciation for the scrupulously traditional techniques that the Nikka founder applied. I also spent time drinking beer and eating *gyutan* (beef tongue), the most famous food specialty of Miyagi Prefecture, with the group.

During the Sendai YLP, one of the American participants was frustrated with the program. After several days of "study hall" to prepare for group presentations, she wanted to try a different format. Dr. Cho was committed to his initial plan, and he asked me to sit down with her to talk her out of it. I did so, though I'm not sure how things ended up after I left.

Over the years, my YLP experiences, meetings with Dr. Cho, and attendance at other events he hosted in Hawai'i, gave me a profound respect for his tireless pursuit of harmony in Northeast Asia. He dedicated his whole life to the proposition that when different people come together and share their cultures and their knowledge, their countries would take one step closer to each other, and that eventually countries tied together through these personal and economic relationships would put conflict behind them forever. It now falls to all of us to work hard to realize his dream.

33

MEMORIES FROM THE BISHOP STREET OFFICE

Siobhán Caruso Ng

Walt Whitman, in *Song of Myself, 51,* wrote:
Do I contradict myself?
Very well then I contradict myself,
(I am large, I contain multitudes.)

Dr. Cho contained multitudes, some of which, of course, contradicted others. I can only speak to the parts of him he shared with me, filtered through my own life experiences. I knew him far less than most people, having only met him just under three years before he passed on to the next part of the journey; but even this short time was enough to make an impression. I'm unashamed to say that I miss him.

As is true for many who knew Dr. Cho, the first time we met was over a meal. It was a meeting to talk about the open graduate assistant position that supported the Northeast Asia Economic Forum. My research was on the pragmatic use of address terms in Korean and my understanding of Korean etiquette was entirely academic. Should I pour the tea for him? When he asked what I wanted to order from the dim sum menu, should I politely decline and defer to him? I was nervous and didn't want to make a mistake. I needn't have worried though. I was still nervous throughout the entire meal, but the longer we sat there, the more I began to sense that while Dr. Cho was certainly more formal than most people I had interacted with, I could also see that he had a genuine interest in getting to know me, in sharing stories, and exchanging information. Reading his memoir, I can see where this comes from.

I worked with Dr. Cho from the middle of 2019, until his passing in late 2020. I went into the office three days a week for a total of ten hours. I usually got there about an hour before he did and focused on NEAEF's work—editing manuscripts for publishing, writing reports for funders, chasing down minute financial details. When he came in, he would go into his office and make phone calls, sometimes calling me in to help with a computer-related matter or asking me to research some funding options. At some point during every day we were in the office together, he would call me in and we would sit at one end of the conference table and talk.

I had heard that Dr. Cho was famously stubborn and set in his ways, and that he wanted someone who was going to do as he asked and not try to innovate too much. I heard this in the stories others told of him, but that was not my experience. I remember feeling surprised and validated when he asked my advice on potential changes to NEAEF's meeting structure and the Young Leaders Program. He always entertained my suggestions for changes in processes or wording or technology upgrades. When it became clear that the COVID-19 pandemic was going to prevent the Annual Meeting and the Young Leaders Program from happening, Dr. Cho jumped enthusiastically into the prospect of running a remote meeting. I couldn't help laughing when he logged on the first day of the meeting and "saw" one of his old friends from Japan who was presenting. He was just so excited.

Of all the memories that I have, though, what I remember most fondly are those talks at the conference room table. He enthusiastically taught me "office" Korean and insisted I learned the Chinese characters that formed the basis of more formal Korean. He told stories meant to impart lessons, the importance of 확인 (confirm in Korean), for example. "확인, 확인, 확인!" he said. It rings in my ears! We talked the etymology of Korean, English, Japanese, and Chinese and chuckled together at nerdy language jokes. He gossiped with me, which always left me bemused and laughing.

I think he saw more in me than I did, but then, I think this was a passion that underpinned all of the work that he did in those last years—using the lessons of his unique journey to help others on theirs. This was the whole point of the Young Leaders Program and the Annual Meetings. There is a lot that we cannot agree on he would say, but that shouldn't stop us from working on the things we can work on together. We're not so different from each other, after all. He expected a great deal, which was aggravating when his priorities conflicted with mine, but the respect he showed me was enough motivation for me to sigh and push ahead. I could see what he expected of himself was even greater.

For all of his love of language and wordplay, his regard was not always found in what he said—he often didn't articulate this regard and his criticism could sometimes be harsh. But it was evident to me in what he did. He always nurtured his relationships with a quick phone call or email, often with a visit over a meal. He made sure to check in, even when there wasn't a reason to. He learned that my sons were studying Japanese, so he found two pocket calendars that were written in English and Japanese and set them aside for me. He went out of his way to get a small space heater that I could put under my desk because the office was so cold. These small things are what I remember most. These and, of course, him shuffling into the office every morning wearing a blazer that was slightly too big for his frame and a grin that crinkled his face and truly made me wonder whether he planned to get up to shenanigans that day. Oh, and also, “확인, 확인, 확인!”

About the Author

Dr. Lee-Jay Cho was considered one of Korea's leading scholars, recognized internationally for his prominent academic achievements. Early in his life, Dr. Cho left Korea for the United States to pursue his academic passion for demography and economics, receiving a master's degree in public administration from George Washington University and master's and doctoral degrees in sociology from the University of Chicago. He subsequently earned doctoral degrees in demography and economics from Tokyo University and Keio University in Japan and published over 150 papers and books on demography and economic development, making a continuous effort to realize Korea's national interests through research and education. In 1998, Dr. Cho became Senior Advisor to the East-West Center in Hawaiʻi and founding chair of the Northeast Asia Economic Forum, distinguishing himself by his zeal for integrating his academic achievements and experience in the larger world.

—*Kyunghyang Shinmun*, Korea, 1999

His undaunting desire from youth was to contribute to the development of Korea through outstanding academic and research accomplishments. He passed away on October 31, 2020, due to coronavirus-related complications at the age of 84. His writings are hopeful reflections in the life story of a brilliant scholar on the doorstep of the twenty-first century.